W9-AZT-410

PRESENTED BY

Stan and Laura Blackburn
in honor of
Margaret Blackburn

SMYTHE GAMBRELL
LIBRARY

WESTMINSTER SCHOOLS

OUR POISONED WATERS

OUR POISONED WATERS

EDWARD F. DOLAN

COBBLEHILL BOOKS
Dutton   New York

Copyright © 1997 by Edward F. Dolan
All rights reserved
No part of this book may be reproduced in any form
without permission in writing from the Publisher.

Library of Congress Cataloging-in-Publication Data
Dolan, Edward F., date
Our poisoned waters / Edward F. Dolan.
    p. cm.
Includes bibliographical references and index
Summary: Examines the serious problem of water pollution in both
fresh and salt water bodies throughout the world and describes what
is being done about it.
ISBN 0-525-65220-5
1. Water—Pollution—Juvenile literature. [1. Water—Pollution.
2. Pollution.] I. Title.
TD422.D65 1997
363.739'4—dc21 96-47175 CIP AC

Published in the United States by Cobblehill Books,
an affiliate of Dutton Children's Books,
a division of Penguin Books USA Inc.
375 Hudson Street, New York, New York 10014

Designed by Mina Greenstein
Printed in the United States of America
First Edition   10 9 8 7 6 5 4 3 2 1

CONTENTS

1

THE WORLD'S WATERS— POISONED AND VANISHING

LET'S BEGIN WITH FOUR AGE-OLD FACTS:

Water is the most common substance on earth. Making up everything from the greatest of oceans to the smallest of puddles, and found under the ground and in the atmosphere, it adds up to an awesome volume of more than 326 million cubic miles.

About 97 percent of the earth's water is salty—some 317 million cubic miles of it. The oceans hold most of the salt water, with the next greatest volume being found in glaciers and ice caps for a total of over 7 million cubic miles.

Fresh water makes up but a fraction of the global total— in all, less than 1 percent. There are just over 2 million cubic miles present in lakes, rivers, streams, bays, and under the ground. In addition, The atmosphere contains another 3,100 cubic miles.

We humans, as do other land animals, depend on the scant amount of fresh water to live. About 60 percent of our body weight is made up of water. To survive, we need to take in about two and a half quarts a day, with one and a half quarts coming from the liquids we drink, and the rest from the water content in our foods. If we lose just 12 percent of our body water, we put our lives in jeopardy.

Now let's turn to a modern fact, a potentially lethal one. We of the twentieth century are inflicting terrible damage on our waters—both salt and fresh. In so doing, we are endangering every form of plant and animal life, our own included, that calls this planet home. It is a harm that frightens thoughtful people everywhere, especially when they think of how our life-sustaining fresh waters are suffering.

Why the Harm?

What is causing the trouble? The answer begins with an astonishing fact: the twentieth century has seen the world's population vault from 1.57 billion people in 1900 to more than 5.6 billion today. Presently alive are the most people ever to inhabit the earth at one time, with their number expected to reach the 7.9 billion mark by 2020 and to top out and stabilize itself at between 10 and 12 billion by late in the century.

It's obvious that the more people there are the more fresh water is needed—and not simply for drinking and household tasks. To keep pace with the needs and desires of the ballooning population, farms and industries everywhere have been forced to increase the output of their wares, with industry using more and more fresh water to manufacture more and more goods, and agriculture gobbling up ever-growing amounts to irrigate the millions of acres now required to supply the world with food.

Joining industry and agriculture in the expanded use of fresh water are urban areas everywhere. For their growing populations, they have constructed facilities that carry water to every type of building—from towering skyscrapers to the most modest of homes. They have extended water pipelines out to distant suburban areas. And they have laid down the sewer systems so needed to handle the ugly job of disposing of a mounting flow of human waste, a task vital for the good health of their people.

All these efforts—and many others—have been needed and welcomed, but today we can see something that escaped the notice of many people earlier in the century. Coming with all the efforts have been problems that have severely damaged the world's fresh waters in two basic ways.

First, many countries, in an effort to satisfy the needs of their people, industries, and farms, are draining their

stores of fresh water at a rate faster than nature can replace them with rain and melting snow. Their water is in
danger of disappearing.

Second, farms have used pesticides to increase their
crop yields; factories have used chemicals to help produce
their wares; and the growing population has created more
refuse than ever seen before. These are all pollutants.
They have all escaped or have been emptied into lakes,
rivers, and oceans, with the result that not only our fresh
waters but also our salt waters have become sullied with
everything from toxic substances to household rubbish
and human excrement.

Let us look for a moment at some of the damage that
is currently being done.

Our Vanishing Fresh Water

The fresh-water supply in many countries is being used
up so quickly that, unless the brakes are applied, it will
have all but vanished by the mid-twenty-first century. The
countries will be left with so little fresh water that they
may be unable to survive.

The supply is being exhausted in several ways. For one,
of course, it is being called on for daily use by more people
than ever before in the history of our planet. They are all
demanding a share for drinking, cooking, bathing, and
washing clothes. In addition, countless people in the advanced societies are tapping the supply for such luxuries
as private swimming pools, hot tubs, lawn sprinkler sys-

tems, and clothes and dish washers. The situation has already caused the fresh-water supply to drop by one-third per person in many parts of the world.

Though people are demanding a growing share of the world's fresh water, agriculture is demanding the greatest share. It is using a staggering percentage for irrigation. Today, irrigation claims most of the water that is removed each year from the world's lakes, rivers, streams, and underground sources—65 percent (just about two-thirds) in all, leaving only 35 percent for industrial, household, and all other purposes. In California, the percentage of the state's fresh water taken for irrigation is even greater—a whopping 85 percent.

Another harm has emerged from the places where increasing numbers of people have gone to live. In many instances, they have chosen spots that do not have enough water to meet their needs. In the United States, a major California city serves as a ready case in point.

Los Angeles sprawls over a coastal desert that has a local water supply sufficient for about 1 million people—the number who lived there before World War II. But, in the decades since the war, the city's population has exploded to more than 14 million. There simply is not enough water for everyone, and so Los Angeles has been forced to bring in increasing amounts of water from points hundreds of miles away—mainly from northern California and the Colorado River. The removal from those distant points has deprived *their* people of much of the water needed for their own farms, factories, and homes.

Los Angeles is not the only place that ships in water

from great distances. Engineers throughout the world have diverted rivers from their ancient courses so that their waters, as in the case of Los Angeles, can travel via canals and pipelines to distant farms, factories, and cities. The results of these diversions have been both happy and disastrous. In the United States, industries are now spread across the country rather than concentrated in specific areas. The towns and cities in which they stand have prospered. Farms are now found in regions that would still be what they once were—barren lands—were it not for the irrigation water that has flowed into them.

But the diverting of the rivers has damaged them and the lakes and oceans into which they flow. They have also suffered from the dams that have been built not just to divert the rivers but also to provide flood control and store water for use during dry seasons and droughts.

The Polluted Waters

Both our fresh and salt waters suffer from pollution. Filth pours daily into the coastal waters of the oceans (the waters at mid-ocean remain pretty clean) and into lakes, rivers, and streams across the world. It comes mainly from farms employing the pesticides that enhance crop yields but that mingle with the irrigation water to flow into nearby waters via drainage systems; from factories using chemicals that are pumped away from the factory sites; and from sewage systems disposing of their wastes. All these pollutants can also enter the waters with the runoffs that follow rain and snow.

Accidents are responsible for a share of the pollution. They occur frequently, as witness a pair that happened within two months of each other. In late November, 1989, some 18,000 fish were killed when a liquid form of chicken manure that contained a heavy amount of ammonia was accidentally released into a small river in western Missouri; the liquid was used for irrigation and escaped when a spraying machine malfunctioned and leaked for several days before its problem was discovered. Then, in the following January, about 10,000 gallons of unleaded gasoline poured into the Monongahela River upstream of Pittsburgh, Pennsylvania, when a barge struck a bridge and broke open.

Joining all else in creating trouble is the carelessness of the world's litterers, all those people who refuse to take their trash home but lazily drop it in gutters and alongside roadways, there to find its way into sewage and drainage systems—or along beaches, there to be pulled into the surf and then disgorged again by the ebb and flow of the tides.

The harm can be seen throughout the United States. Consider just one example of what is happening to the country's fresh water. In 1989, the Environmental Protection Agency (EPA) reported that the waste products from surrounding cities, towns, farms, and industries had polluted at least 17,365 lakes, rivers, and streams. The wastes consisted mainly of the pollutants in sewage systems, the toxins in drainage systems (among them, the agricultural pesticides), and the residues left behind in manufacturing (from solvents to metals). The polluted waterways make up about 10 percent of all United States waters. (The EPA is the federal agency that is charged with sighting, monitoring, and solving the nation's environmental problems.)

And what of America's salt waters? In 1993, the federal government reported that, during the preceding year, more than 2,600 beaches along all its coasts had been closed to swimming or had been posted with warnings against swimming due to the filth in the water. Blamed for most of the closings were high levels of bacteria that had been generated by the garbage and other pollutants being cast overboard from ships or pumped into the sea from sewage and drainage systems.

But it is unfair to speak just of America's problems. Here are a few examples of the pollution found beyond our shores.

In Europe, the wastes and contaminants from sixteen nations flood into the Black Sea, reaching their destination via a system of 300 rivers and streams. The Black Sea, which is slightly larger than the state of California, once netted marvelous catches for Europe's fish markets and provided jobs for some 2 million fishermen and fishery workers. Now, because of the pollution, it is currently well on its way to becoming a dead body of water. Its fish are threatened with extinction. Its beaches are so befouled that they are shunned by visitors and residents alike, badly depleting a once highly profitable tourist industry.

And just how poisoned are the rivers that are killing the Black Sea? One of its principal feeders, the Dneiper, contains heavy concentrations of the pesticides used on the surrounding croplands. The Danube, another major feeder, is choked with both industrial and agricultural wastes. Among the poisons it annually dumps into the Black Sea are 60,000 tons of phosphorus, 50,000 tons of oil, 4,500 tons of lead, and 60 tons of mercury.

The tainted rivers to the Black Sea have much company elsewhere in Europe. Badly contaminated, for example, are Poland's waterways. Three-quarters of the nation's rivers have become too polluted even for industrial use.

Next, from across the world comes word that some of the magnificent beaches near Sydney, Australia, must be closed to swimming two or three times a week because of the sewage pouring into the sea from the city.

Still another report speaks of the tragedy that is befalling the coral reefs of Southeast Asia. Ranging from the Philippine Islands and China to Indonesia and beyond, they are being systematically destroyed by a type of fishing. Divers, carrying quart-size bottles of sodium cyanide, move silently among the surrounding sea life and squirt the toxin at the larger fish. The cyanide stuns its victims and makes them easier to capture. Among the prey are such exotic species as the Maori wrasse and the panther grouper. On being brought to the surface, the fish are revived and then shipped to markets throughout Asia, where they are sold fresh. They are considered great delicacies and are in heavy demand, with the Maori wrasse selling for $82 a pound.

The amount of cyanide is not enough to kill the large fish. Nor is the amount left in their bodies sufficient to harm most of the people who eat them. But the same cannot be said of the smaller fish that inhabit the reefs and innocently get in the way. The dosage kills them and other tiny species. Killed, too, is the living coral that makes up the reefs. The ecosystems of the reefs are dying and the reefs themselves, once a kaleidoscope of brilliant colors, are turning a deathly gray.

The dangers that threaten the world's waters—and, as a consequence, ourselves—are great. The picture of what is happening to our fresh-water supplies as we drain them away too quickly, our rivers as we dam them and divert them from their natural courses, and our salt and fresh water bodies as we poison them with pollutants is a bleak one. But, bleak though it may be, the picture is not a hopeless one.

While water problems are to be seen worldwide, they do *not* blanket every square inch of the globe; they pose a terrible threat in many places but not as yet in others, where the water and the life in and around it are still in good health. Further, steps are being taken by public and private bodies at all levels—from the international to the local—and by countless individuals everywhere to rescue and restore the waters already poisoned, to slow the loss of the waters being too quickly drained, and to preserve those that still remain in good health.

Finally, it is a picture that you can help to brighten.

There are many things that you, as a young person now and as an adult in future years, can do to assist all those working to reach the day when everywhere in our country and the world there will be again a clean and adequate supply of water.

2

OUR VANISHING FRESH WATER

You're playing volleyball with friends on a blazing summer day. Your body glistens with perspiration. Everyone decides to take a break and relax under a tree. There, in the shade, your perspiration disappears, leaving your body dry.

Now it is late in a winter's afternoon. You're walking home from school or your part-time job. Heavy dark clouds loom overhead. Suddenly, rain begins to pelt you. You're soaked through to the skin by the time you reach your front door.

These are experiences familiar to us all. We accept them as ordinary occurrences in life. Rarely, if ever, do we take a moment to think of what they really are—demonstrations of the wondrous fact that nature keeps the world's waters endlessly on the move and that their movement provides us with the continuing supply of the fresh water we need for survival. The movement itself is called the *hydrological cycle*.

The Hydrological Cycle

In brief, the cycle sends the world's water—from the oceans, lakes, rivers, streams, puddles, the ground itself, and all plant and animal life—into the sky as vapor, cleanses it, and then transforms it back into water and returns it to earth as precipitation. *Precipitation* is the term for any moisture that falls from the atmosphere. Rain and snow are its most familiar forms. Other forms include drizzle, sleet, and hail.

The cycle begins when the earth, after absorbing the sun's heat, lifts it back into the atmosphere. The heat causes the various moistures at the surface (including the perspiration coating your body that summer day) to evaporate and rise with it.

Once in the atmosphere, the vapor remains there for an average of eleven to twelve days and can travel thousands of miles on the wind before weather conditions release it as precipitation. The cycle constantly repeats itself, annually pulling 97,000 cubic miles of moisture into the air, renewing it, and depositing it back on earth as fresh, clean water.

Of those 97,000 cubic miles, approximately 83,000—about 86 percent—rise from the oceans (as is to be expected since the seas cover some 70 percent of the earth's surface), with the remaining 14 percent coming from all other sources. The end of the cycle returns 100 percent of the evaporated moisture. However, it drops the major share—approximately 75 percent—directly into the oceans because of their size. The remaining percentage falls on the land and begins to make its way back to the seas via rivers, streams, lakes, and routes beneath the ground.

In giving us a continuing supply of fresh water, the cycle is a magnificent process of nature. But nature plays a trick on us—and on people everywhere—by drastically reducing the supply everyone receives. Only about a third of the water that returns to the land stays around to be of use as fresh water. Two-thirds evaporates back into the air, is soaked up by plants for their survival, or flows into the seas.

Nature also plays another trick on us. It makes the cycle an unfair process. Why? Because of varying climatic conditions, the cycle does not distribute its rainfall evenly over the world. It blesses the people of some areas with as much or more fresh water than they need. It makes others "water poor" or even "water starved."

A Lucky United States

The United States is among the fortunate countries that the cycle treats kindly. The nation is rich in fresh water. Though there are extensive desert areas in the Southwest that receive little precipitation (five inches or less annually), most of the country enjoys a healthy rainfall, with yearly averages ranging from more than twenty inches in the East and parts of the West to upwards of 100 inches in the Northwest. Further, it abounds with lakes (the Great Lakes, for example, constitute the world's second largest body of fresh water, exceeded in capacity only by Russia's Lake Baikal), rivers, streams, and snow-blanketed peaks that unleash tons of water during spring thaws. In addition, the United States has a splendid supply of ground water.

Ground water is water that soaks into the earth during the cycle and is pulled toward the seas by gravity, flowing through cracks, caverns, and porous rock formations en route. Much of it becomes trapped in pockets to form underground pools that can be "harvested" for use by drilling wells. In some areas, the pockets are so close to the surface that the local water table lies a mere four inches underfoot. (A water table is defined as the highest level to which ground water rises in a given spot). And some are so close underfoot and so gorged with water that it bursts through the surface to gift us with artesian wells.

An especially rich supply of ground water is found in the nation's *aquifers*. Underlying vast stretches of the country, they are formations of porous rock into which water seeps and is trapped and stored. If an aquifer is close enough to the surface, its waters can be tapped for use. One of America's greatest aquifers is the Ogallala. Hidden beneath a sprawling area in the West, it stretches from South Dakota down to Texas and provides about 30 percent of the ground water used to irrigate the nation's farms, especially those in the arid Southwest. Its waters have transformed vast desert tracts there into flourishing croplands.

Just how lucky the United States is in its fresh water sources can be seen by looking at other parts of the world, especially the Middle East and Africa.

The Middle East and Africa

In her book, *Last Oasis: Facing Water Scarcity*, environmental writer Sandra Postel reports that twenty countries in these two regions, with a combined population of 192.5 million, are so water poor that they face the danger of water starvation—of having too little water for their survival at some point in the twenty-first century. Facing this prospect are:

In the Middle East	In Africa
Bahrain	Algeria
Israel	Botswana
Jordan	Burundi
Kuwait	Cape Verde
Qatar	Djibouti
Saudi Arabia	Egypt
Syria	Kenya
United Arab Emirates	Libya
Yemen	Mauritania
	Rwanda
	Tunisia

Water poorness poses a terrible threat for any nation. It keeps the standard of living of the people low. It throttles the country's industry and agriculture, leading to widespread joblessness and hunger. It can prevent the nation from developing and flourishing. Water starvation, as we'll see, can do far worse.

Responsible for the plight of the twenty countries are two basic factors. First, they all suffer a meager annual rainfall. In Africa, for example, Egypt receives about eight inches a year in its rainiest area, which lies along the Mediterranean coast, with far less falling in the interior. Mauritania averages seven inches in some areas, and less than four in others. Kenya has as little as four in many spots. Over in the neighboring Middle East, Saudi Arabia also averages four inches, but has a desert—the Rub' al Khali—that often goes without a drop for ten years.

The second factor is the growth of their populations. In the past, they may have been water poor with their miserly rainfall, but they were not water starved. Their populations were small and, though great care had to be taken to conserve the water supply, it was usually adequate for the number of people it served. Aiding it were other sources that offset the lack of rain—for one, their aquifers; for another, the ground water that fed town wells and desert oases; and, for still another, the great rivers that, often swollen with runoff, flowed through some of the countries from neighboring lands. In Africa, for example, there is the Nile, whose annual flooding with water from the regions upstream made ancient Egypt the richest of agricultural nations.

But, throughout the twentieth century, in common with the rest of the world, the populations of the twenty countries have steadily mounted. Today, they are surging past the point where they can be handled comfortably by their local water supplies.

Water starvation is fast becoming a terrible fact of life for the twenty because they are all expected to double their populations sometime early in the twenty-first century. Saudi Arabia, presently the home of 16 million people, will have twice that number in twenty years unless its rate of growth is slowed. So will Jordan with its current 1.4 million people. Egypt's population (now 55 million) is expected to double in twenty-eight years; and Kenya (26 million) and Mauritania (2 million) in twenty-five.

With little rain and a continuing population explosion on their hands, the countries are tapping their aquifers and other ground water stores to meet their current needs—and hastening the day of water starvation by over-tapping them.

The Disappearing Aquifers

To understand how dangerous this overtapping is we need to make a point about the aquifers. They differ from rain water in a significant way. Rain water is called a renewable source because it is constantly returned by the hydrological cycle for further use. But the aquifers are known as nonrenewable sources. The term is misleading because they are replenished by rainfall and the runoff from rain and melting snow. But, located deep beneath the surface, they are replenished at an agonizingly slow rate due to the time it takes the water to seep down to and then settle in their porous structures. Pumping water from them is like mining coal. Once the coal is removed, it is gone for good. For all practical purposes, the same holds true for the aquifer water; once gone, it's the same as being gone for good because thousands of years will be needed for more water to trickle down and replace it. Any aquifer must always be pumped at a rate that will give it as much time as possible to rebuild itself.

Care must also be taken in withdrawing the other forms of ground water for use. They, too, need time to rebuild themselves, especially in countries with scant rainfalls, and so must not be drained at a rate faster than their water can be replaced.

But such care is not being exercised in the many of the water-poor countries. For example, Saudi Arabia depends on its aquifers for 75 percent of its water needs and is presently pumping them out at the rate of 1.4 billion cubic feet per year. The water is not only meant for use by the people but also for the irrigation of a crop that the government considers all-important. Some two decades ago, the Saudis decided to become self-sufficient in wheat. They reached that goal in the mid-1980s and, with enough wheat to serve their own needs, have gone on to become one of the world's leading exporters of the grain, doing so at a high cost in fresh water. Today, Saudi Arabia's aquifers are being used to irrigate an annual wheat crop of 2 to 4 million tons, with 1,000 tons of water needed to produce a single ton of the crop.

The rate of pumping has steadily increased in the 1990s. Hydrologists have warned the Saudis that, unless the rate of withdrawal is slowed, their aquifer water will all but disappear in the next fifty years—or sooner if the country decides to speed things up.

What will happen when the supply is exhausted? Even with the great wealth that its oil resources reap, Saudi Arabia will face a string of economic problems. First, it may have to go to the expense of building more desalination plants to help meet its needs; these plants provide fresh water by removing the salt from seawater, and Saudi Arabia already has several dotting its Persian Gulf coastline. Next, with less water at hand for irrigation, the country's wheat yields will dwindle, forcing it to rely increasingly on imports of the grain.

Finally, it will assuredly be forced to import water from great distances by ship or pipeline. One possibility is the purchase of water from Turkey, where the mighty Tigris and Euphrates rivers take shape. The Turkish government, which is currently building major dam and irrigation projects on the two rivers, is thinking about laying down hundreds of miles of pipeline to feed Saudi Arabia and its fellow water-poor states, among them Syria, Jordan, Kuwait, and the United Arab Emirates. The pipeline construction will cost an estimated $21 billion, and so the price of its water will be high, perhaps backbreakingly high.

Or there could be war should Saudi Arabia become desperate enough to turn on its neighbors and try to grab their meager water supplies. In today's small world, that war could spread far afield and become an international conflict.

If you think that the idea of a war breaking out over water is farfetched, think again. The Nile River provides water for nine countries as it flows north to the Mediterranean from its wellsprings in Burundi and Ethiopia. Egypt is the last of the nine to receive its largesse and is so deeply concerned by the loss of the river's waters to its neighbors that its political leaders have threatened them with war if they try to take more.

Water may be known for its ability to put out fires, but it also has the power to ignite the very worst of blazes.

Aquifer Loss Elsewhere

Saudi Arabia is not the only nation quickly depleting its aquifer and other ground waters. The same depletion is being seen in India, China, and Thailand. In the western hemisphere, it is happening in Mexico and in the Southwestern United States. They are all pumping the water out at a rate many times faster than the hydrological cycle can replace it. In China, the level of ground water beneath the city of Beijing (Peking) is dropping between three and six feet a year; city officials are predicting that, by the dawn of the twenty-first century, Beijing and its surrounding countryside will need 70 percent more water than it can supply. The draining of the aquifer water at Mexico City now exceeds the replacement speed by 50 to 80 percent. If these regions continue to pump at the present rate, their fresh-water supply simply cannot last much longer than a few decades.

The situation in Mexico City is especially desperate. Originally built by the Aztecs centuries ago, the city first stood on an island in one of a series of interconnected lakes. They provided the Aztecs with a wealth of fresh water, but that situation changed soon after the Spanish conquered Mexico. The newcomers began to drain the lakes to irrigate the country's farms. In time, the lakes ran dry, and the city was eventually forced to pump its water from the aquifers that lay beneath it.

The pumping has increased in recent decades due to the city's multiplying population (now an astounding 20 million) and its growing industrial work (carried on in more than 40,000 factories). Consequently, so much water has been withdrawn that weak spots—sinkholes—have been left behind. Unable to bear the weight above them, they have begun to give way and the city is now subsiding into them. Homes, buildings, streets, and historic monuments are sinking at the rate of four inches a year in some spots to more than a foot in others. In the city's main plaza, the great stone Metropolitan Cathedral, which was built by the Spanish in the 1500s, is now tilted over to its right because of the severe sinkage on that side.

Years ago, when city officials first noticed the sinking, they began to build giant aqueducts to bring water in from the outside. Today, Mexico City's water supply comes mainly from Valle del Bravo sixty miles away and is pumped along a course that lifts it 3,000 feet before it reaches its destination. The import system has not proved to be a solution to the city's water problem because it burdens the people with water bills too costly for them to meet. The municipal government must help them by paying a staggering $125 million a year in water costs.

Consequently, Mexico City is faced daily with two questions. How long can its government bear such an annual cost? How long can it continue to sink before the home of 20 million people becomes uninhabitable? The questions are frightening. The answers, unless Mexico City can find a solution to its water problem, are even more frightening.

The Ogallala Threat

In the American Southwest, severe harm is being done to the Ogallala aquifer, which spreads south from South Dakota to Texas and fans out to a number of other states— among them Colorado, New Mexico, and Nebraska. In the decades since it was first tapped, it has transformed vast Southwestern desert tracts into fertile croplands that produce fruits, vegetables, melons, and grains—especially grains for the cattle industry in Texas.

But to meet the demands of the Southwest's agriculture, industry, and people, the Ogallala is being drained at a dangerous rate. Over the past fifty years, the expanse of the aquifer beneath Texas has given up 24 percent of its water. Overall, the Ogallala is being drained at a rate fifty times faster than newly arriving water can seep down into its confines. Unless the rate slows, it will be completely dry under New Mexico by the year 2020 and will be dangerously low virtually everywhere south of Nebraska.

If and when the Ogallala is finally drained, the Southwest will be in much the same trouble as the future Saudi Arabia. Though the region, as it does now, will be able to draw water from the Colorado and Rio Grande rivers, there will certainly be a decline in its crop output (this has already happened in parts of Texas) and industrial production. Vast expanses of the Southwest might return to the arid desert lands they once were as farms and industries close and people move to more hospitable areas.

Other Dangers

The loss of fresh water that will take centuries to replace is not the only damage being done to the over-pumped aquifers. In Mexico City, in addition to creating sinkholes, the city's pumping has caused the subterranean layer above the aquifers to dry out and crack. In times past, that layer had sealed them from the surface and had prevented contaminants from seeping into them. But no longer. Industrial and other pollutants are now making their way into the underground stores and beginning to poison them. Water officials say that, once the aquifers are poisoned, it will be economically backbreaking to cleanse them. The pollution will be irreversible and the city will be vulnerable to an increasing rate of intestinal diseases, among them dysentery.

An exactly opposite problem has struck California's Central Valley, whose vegetable, fruit, and grain crops make it one of the nation's most valued agricultural regions. The pumping of its aquifers has caused their porous formations to compact—press together—and deprive the incoming water of the avenues it needs to seep into them. As a result, the Valley has lost nearly 88 billion cubic feet of water storage space in recent years.

Still another problem: The draining of coastal aquifers worldwide has opened the way for seawater to seep into them and taint their water with salt, making it unfit for drinking and agriculture. This problem is readily seen along the Mediterranean shores of Israel, where the invasion of salt water is causing hydrologists to predict that 20 percent of the nation's coastal wells will be unusable within a few years.

Though the hydrological cycle gives us an unending source of fresh water, it is a very limited one. Unless we take care with our ground and aquifer waters, our freshwater supply could soon disappear, perhaps not totally but certainly to the point where there would not be enough for us to live our lives as we do today. Food and industrial production would suffer, cities could be forced to make water available for just a few hours daily, and hydroelectric power could be curtailed. On a very personal level, cars could not be washed whenever we wished, toilets could not be flushed after every use (as was the case during the drought that struck parts of the United States in the 1980s), and children could not dash happily through lawn sprinklers on a summer day.

Sadly, we are doing far more today than depleting the waters that lie out of sight beneath our feet. We are harming our water supply in yet another way. We now turn to what we are doing to our surface fresh waters, beginning with our rivers.

3

ENDANGERED RIVERS

WE DAMAGE OUR RIVERS when we interfere with and change their nature and their natural way of doing things. When left alone, they provide the water we need for survival, serve as habitats for multitudes of fish, birds, animals, and insects, and nourish the countless trees and plants that take root in or alongside them.

But disturb the rivers and the work they have been doing since the beginning of time and trouble quickly follows. The trouble occurs when, first, we divert them from their age-old courses or dam them so that they can be made to perform various tasks for us. The trouble then mounts as we poison them with agricultural and industrial contaminants and inadequately treated sewage.

First, let's look at the ecological problems that can take shape with the diversion and damming of rivers. Later, we'll see how we are poisoning not only our rivers but also *all* our waters, both fresh and salt.

We begin with the disaster that occurred when engineers decided to keep two rivers from entering one of the world's greatest inland seas.

The Dying Aral Sea

Lying in a southern region of the former Soviet Union and surrounded by arid lands, the Aral Sea was for eons the world's fourth largest body of fresh water. Then, a little less than forty years ago, it began to lose that ranking. It was condemned to death to help meet the agricultural needs of the Soviet Union's 289 million people.

It received its death sentence when the government decided to tap the waters of the two great rivers that have flowed into it since time immemorial—the Syr Darya, which enters from the east, and the Amu Darya, which makes its way up from the south. (*Darya* is the Soviet word for river.) The ambitious plan called for their waters to be sent via canals and pipelines to irrigate 18 million arid acres and turn them into a fertile expanse for farming.

As an agricultural project meant to help feed the Soviet population, the tapping proved to be a magnificent success. In time, those 18 million acres were yielding rich harvests in fruits, vegetables, grains, and cotton—in all, over 30 percent of the Soviet Union's fruits, 25 percent of its vegetables, about half its rice, and an amazing 90 percent of its cotton.

But the tapping spelled disaster for the Aral Sea. Between 1960 and the early 1990s, the flow from the Syr Darya and Amu Darya died to a trickle. The Sea—which once measured 280 miles long by 130 miles wide and encompassed 25,400 square miles—shrank by more than 40 percent, leaving behind vast tracts of exposed earth, muddy in some places, dry and caked in others. Today, the shrinkage can be most dramatically seen in the town of Muynak. It was once a fishing port on the Sea. It now lies over thirty miles from the water's edge.

The Soviet officials had the best of intentions in mind when they decided on the irrigation project. If they stopped to think of the damage that the Aral Sea might sustain, they obviously felt it would be far outweighed by the good that would be done. But, as has happened elsewhere in the world when the natural state of things is disturbed, they harmed everything and everyone in the area—from the Sea itself to the crops that the irrigation made possible.

Damage Everywhere

The list of those harms begins with the term *salinization*. Salinization is the process by which salt builds up in the soil. It is most widely seen in irrigated areas.

All water contains some dissolved salt and, when excessive amounts of water are used for irrigation, the salt gathers in the soil and eventually becomes a whitish substance that is seen on the surface. The salt that collected in the Aral's farmlands was carried along in the waters that made their way back to the Sea and its two rivers. The rivers became dangerously salty for drinking and for sustaining their waterlife.

Adding to the tragedy were the pesticides used on the irrigated fields. They, too, were carried back to the two rivers and the Aral. There, environmental writer Sandra Postel reports in the 1996 issue of *State of the World* (a book issued annually by Worldwatch Institute, an organization that tracks environmental problems throughout the globe), they combined with the salt to kill some twenty of the twenty-four species of fish in the Aral. She adds that, in the 1950s, the total fish catch in the Sea came to 44,000 tons and provided 16,000 people with jobs. Now the once-thriving industry has dwindled to almost nothing and the seaside is dotted with abandoned fishing villages.

Suffering with the fish have been trees and birds. They had flourished in the wetlands that the Syr Darya and Amu Darya formed at the points where they entered the Sea. Those wetlands have slowly dried over the years. Lost in the process have been the tamarisk and willow forests that they had long nourished. And lost have been the waterfowl that once flocked to them, either killed by the salt and pesticides or driven away by the inhospitable dryness. Postel reports that, in three decades, the number of the Aral's nesting bird species has dropped from an estimated 173 to a mere 38.

Even the crops that the irrigation made possible have not escaped harm. A dust consisting of salt and the pesticides used to protect them now lies on the Aral's exposed seabed. Each year, heavy winds scoop it up and strew it over the surrounding farmlands. Harmed or destroyed are many of the crops.

The People of the Aral

Thousands of its people have abandoned the Aral region to seek a living elsewhere; the former port of Muynak once boasted a population of 40,000, but now is home to just 12,000. Those who have remained alongside the Sea have suffered an increase in disease due to drinking contaminated water and living with poor sanitary conditions. The incidence of typhoid fever is thirty times as great as in the past, and the incidence of hepatitis (an inflammation of the liver) is seven times as great. The people of Muynak fall prey to cancer of the esophagus (the muscular tube that extends from the throat to the stomach) at a rate fifteen times as great as the Soviet average.

Isaac Asimov and Frederik Pohl, in their book *Our Angry Earth*, explain that the people try to protect themselves by boiling their drinking water, but that even then it is not fit for human consumption. Many freeze the water into cubes, after which they break the cubes open and pour out the concentration of salt and pesticides in the center. Then they melt and drink what is left of the cubes.

The disaster that has befallen the Aral Sea and its surrounding croplands because of salinization has been matched elsewhere. Today, in China, India, Iraq, Pakistan, and South America there are barren lands where no crops will grow. They were once thriving, well-irrigated lands—until salinization crept onto the scene. So was the great ancient civilization of Sumeria. With its lands fed by the Euphrates River (flowing now through Turkey, Syria, and Iraq), Sumeria developed into a prosperous agricultural society, only to collapse around 2000 B.C., in great part because of a lethal buildup of salt in its soil.

The United States needs to pay attention to the Aral's fate. Some areas of our Southwest that are irrigated by the Colorado and Rio Grande rivers are experiencing a heavy increase of salt in the soil.

Dams

Dams are among the oldest of man-made structures. They have been with us since antiquity, storing water behind their walls so that it can be released to serve a region's economy and people during dry times of the year and periods of drought. They have been used for centuries to provide flood control, and, in modern times, their waters have been put to work generating hydroelectric power. The lakes that have taken shape behind their walls have been employed for everything from bathing and fishing to the pleasure boating and waterskiing seen today on Lake Mead behind America's Hoover Dam.

Quite rightly, dams have long been praised as engineering marvels—and they truly are. But, along with the benefits they have provided, they have caused environmental damage. What they have done can be quickly seen in one of the most modern dams—the Aswan High Dam that straddles Egypt's Nile River.

The Aswan High Dam

The dam was constructed in the 1960s to stem the rush of the Nile during the rainy season and then to release the trapped waters when they are needed for irrigation in the dry seasons. Its waters were sent out to irrigate more than 1 million acres and succeeded in adding 900,000 acres of desert area to Egypt's farmlands. While awaiting release, the waters are stored in the lake that the project created. Christened Nasser Lake—in honor of the late Gamal Abdel Nasser, who served as Egypt's president from 1956 to 1970—it stretches for some 300 miles south along the Nile.

But just what harm has the dam done? Prior to its construction, silt flowed freely along the Nile to the Mediterranean Sea during flood times. As the river approached the sea, the silt fanned out to create one of the most fertile deltas in the world. Today, however, the Aswan's walls trap the silt. As a result, the delta is beginning to diminish in size. In some areas, lying only nine feet or so above sea level, it gives the impression of disappearing as the Mediterranean invades it. Further, the encroaching sea is bringing salt that is despoiling the land. The decrease in the nutrient-rich silt has also had a tragic effect on the health of the coastal marine life and has all but wiped out the saltwater fishing industries—chief among them the sardine industry—in the eastern Mediterranean.

In addition, the dam has created a health problem for the people who live nearby. The silt that piles up behind it breeds disease-causing microbes, parasites, and insects that would flow away were the dam not there. They are

born of the sewage and fertilizers that arrive from towns
and farms upstream. Due to a parasite that is exuded by
small snails in the water, nearly 100 percent of the nearby
people suffer from schistosomiasis, an illness that is
marked by anemia (a deficiency in the quantity or quality
of the blood) and diarrhea. It can be contracted by swimming in or drinking the infected water. It is sometimes
fatal.

The Colorado River Problems

Many problems like those created by the Aswan High
Dam can be seen in the United States when tracing the
course of the Colorado River from its birthplace in the
Rocky Mountains southward to Mexico and its final destination, the Gulf of California. There was a time when
the silt from the river formed a rich delta land at the en-
trance to the Gulf. But today, ten dams—among them the
Glen Canyon, Hoover, Parker, and Imperial dams—loom
along the Colorado's path and divert its waters to serve
the agricultural, industrial, and municipal needs of seven
surrounding states (including Texas, Arizona, and California). By the time the river reaches Mexico and the Gulf,
it is nothing more than a trickle. The delta is drying out.
Salt is creeping into it from the Gulf and the number of
its fish is dwindling. Its wildlife is disappearing as waterfowl and animals—ranging from quail and raccoons to
deer and bobcats—depart in search of happier feeding and
breeding grounds. Families who have farmed the delta
for centuries can no longer grow their crops in the salt-

poisoned soil. Many are being forced to leave the region and seek their livelihoods elsewhere.

The story of the people of the delta is repeated throughout the world wherever the courses of rivers are dammed or the course of their flow diverted. When the rivers reach their destinations in a trickle, there is a decline in the fish and animal life there and a decline in farming as the buildup of salt turns the land barren. The situation is seen at the mouth of the Ganges in India, the Yellow River (Huang He) in China, and the Jordan in Israel.

Solving a Problem

The desire for irrigation water was behind the diverting of the Syr Darya and Amu Darya rivers and the damming of the Nile and Colorado rivers. The same holds true for many other river projects. And for the heavy use of Saudi Arabian, Chinese, Mexican, and American aquifer water.

Agricultural irrigation consumes a staggering percentage of the fresh water that is put to use each year—65 percent in all. Sadly, a great share of that percentage does the crops no good whatsoever. It consists of water that evaporates, flows away accidentally, or seeps into the ground before reaching them.

Agricultural scientists have been working for years to solve these problems. Their aim has been twofold—first, to find ways to use less water without lowering crop yields and, second, to cut down on the amount of water that has always been lost through evaporation and the useless premature seepage into the ground.

The Surge System: This system employs the furrows that are plowed for planting, but with a difference. Instead of letting the water flow into them all at the same time, farmers alternate the flows between two rows at a time. When the water in the first flow seeps into the ground, it tends to "seal" the earth, with the result that the water in the second flow travels more quickly along the furrows and reaches a greater number of plants. The system cuts the loss of water by up to 15 percent.

The Drip System: Developed in dry and hot Israel in the late 1940s, the drip system is now used in countries across the world, among them Australia, Mexico, and the United States. A system of pipes is laid between the rows of plantings, either on the surface of the ground or beneath it. The pipes are punctured with holes alongside each planting. As water passes through the pipes, it leaks out of each hole and goes directly to the plant roots. The system enables up to 95 percent of the water to reach the roots.

The third improvement involves a very simple adaptation of the sprinkler systems used by many farmers. The systems have long featured high-pressure sprinklers, which are known to have an efficiency rating of 60 to 70 percent, meaning that from 40 to 30 percent of their water is lost to evaporation and seepage into the ground away from the plant roots. The old high-pressure sprinklers are now being replaced with low-pressure units. The new units have an efficiency rating of about 80 percent.

These modern irrigation techniques are saving the world tons of fresh water. In the United States alone during the past few years, farmers have lowered the annual depletion of Ogallala aquifer water from 7 *billion* cubic feet to 241 *million* cubic feet. That's a yearly drop of 88 percent.

Irrigation depleted the waters of the Aral Sea and the Colorado River delta, and salinization and farm pesticides poisoned them. But there is another significant cause of harm to our waters. All the world's fresh and salt waters are being poisoned by contaminants that are everywhere being poured into them daily.

4

HOW THE WORLD'S WATERS ARE POISONED

THE MAJOR TYPES of contaminants that are being released, either accidentally or deliberately, into the world's fresh and salt waters are: sewage; solid wastes; chemical pollutants, among them the farm pesticides; radioactive materials; and oil.

Some, such as sewage, have been invading the waters ever since the beginning of time. Others, among them the chemical pollutants, are the products of modern science, agriculture, and manufacturing. Still others, including many of the chemical pollutants and oil, are naturally present in the waters to one degree or another.

Sewage

The amount of human waste that enters the world's fresh and salt waters is beyond calculation. Writer Martha Gorman, in her book *Environmental Hazards: Marine Pollution*, gives us a good idea of that amount, however, when she remarks that every American flushes a toilet an average of five times a day, for a total of some 1.25 billion times daily, all year long. Add to that total the number of times that toilets are flushed across the world—plus the sewage that is generated in countries without modern facilities—and the total mass is indeed beyond calculation.

Two types of sewage flow into the waters—treated and untreated. Before being pumped away, treated sewage passes through treatment plants, where much of its solid content is broken down and its chemical content reduced. In all, the treatment plants are meant to purify the sewage as much as possible so that when it is emptied into the ocean or a river, the water will continue to be safe.

Untreated sewage is raw sewage. It enters the waters without first passing through a treatment plant. Its dangers are great for humans who drink the water into which it flows. It threatens us with viruses that cause dysentery (an inflammation of the intestines), hepatitis (an inflammation of the liver), and the dreaded muscle crippler, poliomyelitis.

Raw sewage also poses a danger for water wildlife. It contains nutrients—various organic and chemical substances—that, on entering the water, trigger a massive increase in the plants, fish, and organisms there. When they later die, they descend to the bottom and decompose. The decomposition of so much matter causes the amount of oxygen in the water to decrease to the point where the living flora and fauna begin to suffocate to death at an accelerating rate.

This deadly process is called *eutrophication*, which comes from the Greek word *eutrophos*, meaning nourishing. In the absence of raw sewage, eutrophication takes place naturally in lakes, ponds, and slow-moving streams when runoffs send other nutrients from the surrounding lands into the waters.

Eutrophication can take centuries or even thousands of years to occur naturally. Raw sewage, however, hastens the process greatly and can bring it about in a matter of months or a few years. So do farm fertilizers, some industrial wastes, and even household detergents. They all contain nutrients, chiefly phosphorus and nitrogen, that breed life in the water too fast.

The dangers of raw sewage loom at their greatest in underdeveloped or emerging nations where the sewage systems are antiquated and dilapidated, or where they are few or nonexistent. Americans are fortunate because, in general, U.S. sewage and water systems are modern and well maintained, making the nation's fresh water safe to drink. Much responsible for the safe water are the treatment plants that have been built with the help of government funds provided by the Federal Water Pollution Control Act of 1972 and the Clean Air Act of 1987.

But make no mistake. The United States, though its drinking water ranks among the world's best, is not without its problems. Bacteria, viruses, and toxic substances often get into its drinking water via the country's treatment and water systems. A 1993 issue of *Time* magazine reported that, in 1989 and 1990, over 4,200 people in sixteen states fell sick, and four died, from bacteria and viruses in their drinking water. Accounting for some of the trouble is the fact that, despite the 1972 and 1987 Acts, the United States still has many treatment plants that are old and in need of replacement or upgrading. Some suffer the problem of having raw sewage escape when their tanks and ponds overflow during heavy storms.

In 1996, Congress took a major step towards alleviating these problems when it enacted the Safe Drinking Water Act. The measure requires water systems to report yearly to the public on the bacteria and pollutants found in tap water, to describe how such contaminants can affect the health of users, and to control the most dangerous of the pollutants. (Some states already require water systems to notify customers when pollutants are discvovered.) Congress hopes the measure will serve as an incentive to water systems to maintain good water quality. In addition, the Act provides over $9 billion for grants and loans to states for the upgrading of their water facilities.

Solid Wastes

Any discarded item with three dimensions qualifies as solid waste. Consequently, the solid wastes are of all types and sizes. They range from sunken ships to garbage, radios, car batteries, paint cans, strips of wood, and toys.

Solid wastes can enter the water in any number of ways. In they go when pleasure boats, freighters, and cruise ships dump them overboard, either accidentally or deliberately. In they go when picnickers carelessly toss aside their soft drink cans on a riverbank or along the seashore, there to drift into the water with the wind or to be pulled in by the tide. And in they go when caught in a runoff.

Perhaps the greatest number of solid waste items today are made of plastic, which has become the late century's most popular man-made substance, replacing so much of the wood, paper, metal, and glass of yesteryear. The list of plastic wastes seems endless. At one end of the scale are giant nets and lines that have broken away from fishing boats. At the other end are shopping bags, purses, bottles, food and candy wrappers, picnic ware, and disposable diapers.

Plastic wastes are a particular threat to both fresh and salt-water life. Each year they are responsible for the deaths of millions of ocean creatures, from marine birds and fish to seals, otters, and sea turtles.

If the manufacture of all plastic products were to stop today, those already in the water would go on killing for years to come, this because, unlike many other types of solid waste, plastic takes a long while to disintegrate. Plastic sandwich bags can survive for fifty years. Plastic bottle caps, dishware, and parts of electrical appliances need several centuries to degrade and disappear. Some plastics, such as polystyrene, can linger on for 500 years or more.

Chemical Pollutants

We live in a universe of chemicals. They go into the manufacture of a host of commercial products and serve as farm pesticides. Some are harmless and some toxic. Among the most widely used of the toxic chemicals are the heavy metals.

Heavy Metals

Heavy metals occur naturally in the environment. They are found in the earth's crust and the ocean. Among the former are calcium, iron, magnesium, mercury, potassium, and sodium. Metals such as cobalt, manganese, selenium, and tin are also found in the oceans. Contained within our bodies are certain of the heavy metals. For example, we all carry small amounts of potassium, iron, and calcium in our systems.

All the heavy metals—with the exception of mercury— are essential for the maintenance of life. They are not health threats in small amounts, but they become dangerous when they collect in the water, the earth, and the atmosphere, and then enter our bodies in greater-than-normal amounts through breathing, eating, and drinking. Especially dangerous in heavy concentrations are mercury, cadmium, lead, and copper. In industry, mercury is used in the production of plastics; cadmium in metal plating and car batteries; and lead also in car batteries.

During manufacture, the heavy metals leave behind a residue that is piped into nearby waters or that escapes into the atmosphere from factory smokestacks and then is returned to the land and the waters in rain. Some lose a percentage of their contents as they are being mined, after which runoffs carry them into the water.

High concentrations of the heavy metals can lead to

disaster for water life, as witness what happened to the Netherlands in the 1950s, when a Dutch industry released great amounts of copper sulfate into the country's coastal waters. The sea was expected to render the sulfate harmless by dispersing it over a vast area, but it failed to do so, with the chemical remaining on the scene to kill more than 100,000 fish.

The harms that the heavy metals can do to humans are many. High levels of mercury or lead upset the nervous system. Cadmium attacks the liver and kidneys and, in time, replaces the calcium in the bones; the calcium loss in some victims causes the bones to become so brittle that a bout of coughing will break them. Copper can cause jaundice (a liver disease that turns the skin yellow) and cirrhosis of the liver (the destruction of the liver cells).

The Dangerous Halogens

The halogens (from the Greek meaning "salt producers") are members of a family of chemicals that includes bromine, chlorine, fluorine, and iodine. When they are mixed with various organic substances, they become known as organo-halogens. As such, they serve in bleaching products, pesticides, herbicides, solvents, fire retardants, and as raw materials in the manufacture of plastics.

One of the organo-halogen pesticides is kepone. In the early 1970s, its presence in agricultural runoffs so polluted Virginia's James River that the waterway had to be closed to fishing from 1975 to late 1980. It was also banned on parts of Chesapeake Bay into which the James flows.

Making up a major branch of the organo-halogen family

are the dioxins. These are various chemical compounds that take shape when the organo-halogens are being brewed for use in the manufacture of herbicides, wood preservatives, paper, and other products. The dioxins then remain on the scene as contaminants. They are found in the waters into which paper mills dump their wastes and are suspected of causing maladies that range from rashes to nerve damage and birth defects.

PCBs (*polychlorinated biphenyls*) rank as another dangerous arm of the organo-halogen family. They are mixtures of chlorine and hydrocarbons and they serve in the manufacture of electrical, adhesive, and plastic products. They escape into the atmosphere, bodies of water, and food in a variety of ways, most often by escaping when factories are disposing of their manufacturing wastes. When they are inhaled or eaten by humans, they can cause dizziness, nausea, brochitis, and skin and eye problems.

During a six-year period at one time, they were pumped into the upper Hudson River from two electrical plants in such heavy amounts (a total of 640,000 pounds) and so poisoned the river fish that commercial fishing was banned there for many years and is just now beginning to return.

Radioactive Materials

Radioactive materials play a role in all aspects of the production of nuclear energy. They include substances, such as uranium, which are themselves radioactive, and materials that become radioactive during the production process. These materials are designated as radioactive wastes and must be set aside for disposal. They range from the water used as a coolant during production to the gloves worn by nuclear workers.

In sufficient amounts, radioactive materials are dangerous to the health of all plants, animals, and humans. The danger lies in the rays they radiate. Consequently, every facility that deals in nuclear work must take steps to protect its people and the public from the rays. For example, some of the most dangerous radioactivity is to be found in the fuel assemblies that are placed in the reactors at electrical power plants. Their fuel drives the reactors and, once it is spent, the assemblies are shot through with radioactivity. They must be removed by remote handling, with no one touching them directly, and then stored in ways that prevent their radiation from escaping—namely, in concrete or lead containers or tanks of water.

Though precautions are taken to protect us from the radioactive materials, they have found their way into the world's waters ever since the birth of the nuclear age in the 1940s. This was particularly true early on, when their dangers were not yet fully understood. The surface detonations of nuclear weapons—such as early land and sea test explosions and the deadly bombings of Hiroshima and Nagasaki that ended World War II—spewed them into the atmosphere, there to be borne on the winds until falling back to the land and waters in rain. The sea explosions likewise poisoned the surrounding waters while the land explosions contaminated the ground at the test sites, with the soil then giving off a dust that could be carried to the nearby waters via the winds or runoffs. The radioactivity in the soil could also seep downward and infiltrate the area's ground water. Ground water is the water that fills aquifers and provides fresh water for wells. If contaminated with radioactive materials, it is not usable.

Over the decades, nuclear plants, after using water as a coolant, have sometimes discharged it, accidentally or deliberately, into rivers or coastal waters. Radioactive gases, destined to return in rainfalls, have flowed from power plant smokestacks. Some water in the cooling systems in nuclear submarines has always escaped into the sea when the subs are fired up for sailing.

Once born, radioactive materials begin to decay. They remain dangerous until decaying to the point called their half-life. *Half-life* is the term that scientists use to measure the time needed for half the atoms in a radioactive element to lose their radioactivity and leave it safe to handle. The various radioactive elements decay at different speeds. Some drop to safe levels within seconds, minutes, or days. Others arrive there in weeks or months. The radioactivity in some elements, however, requires centuries or thousands of years to reach half-life. One of the most dangerous of the lot, plutonium, needs 250,000 years for the job.

Fortunately, humans have a resistance to radiation because we are bombarded with it daily from the solar ac-

tivity in space. It also reaches us when the naturally radioactive materials on the land and in the water decay.
Because of our natural resistance, medicine is able to di-
agnose illnesses with small amounts of radioactive substances and treat illnesses such as cancer with larger
dosages.

The health problems come when we are hit with very
high dosages, either through inhalation or eating contaminated foods. Then the radioactivity can trigger rashes and
hair loss, cause ulcers in the gastrointestinal tract, and
damage the bone marrow. High dosages, whether coming
all at one time or over an extended period, are strongly
suspected of causing birth defects and various types of
cancer.

Nuclear work produces two types of waste materials—
high-level and low-level wastes. High-level wastes are ex-
tremely dangerous and can best be illustrated by the fuel
assemblies that become shot through with radioactivity
when firing reactors. Low-level wastes are far less hazard-
ous. They consist of such materials as the rags, tools, and
gloves used by nuclear workers.

It is necessary to dispose of each type safely. In the early
days of the nuclear age, the United States and other countries disposed of the wastes by placing them in 55-gallon
steel drums lined with lead and dumping them in the sea,
a practice that caused people throughout the world to fear
that the drums might break open and contaminate the
waters. The United States abandoned the practice in 1971.
Since then, most countries have shunned sea dumping

and have elected to bury the wastes, placing the low-level ones in graves, and the lethal high-level ones in caves or specially built underground vaults. But a widespread fear remains—that the canisters in which the high-level wastes are placed for burial will decay or break open and release the radioactivity into the surrounding earth.

Oil

Oil enters our fresh and salt waters in myriad ways. Nature itself provides a major share of the oil in the oceans. It does so by allowing the oil in the earth's crust to seep into the water via cracks in the seabed. Estimates hold that anywhere from around 50 percent to more than 90 percent of all the oil present in the oceans is there because of natural seepage.

Next, oil flows into rivers and coastal waters when the drippings from cars are swept away from streets and highways by rain, when oil is changed in automobile engines and then poured down drains, and when it is hosed away from factory floors. It gets into the water when tankers wash out their tanks and bilges (a practice now internationally banned but often ignored by ship owners). Its fumes rise into the atmosphere to be caught in rainfall when gasoline and other petroleum products are burned. Finally, it is spilled into the water by accidents involving tankers and offshore drilling rigs.

There are thousands of accidental spills across the

world annually. Many go unnoticed because they involve anything from a few to several thousand gallons that the sea is able to absorb. The major spills—such as the one that happened when the tanker *Exxon Valdez* went aground in Alaska's Prince William Sound in 1989—release millions of black gallons and make headlines everywhere.

They earn headlines because, of all the spills, they do the greatest and most readily seen harm to the waters, shores, and wildlife. Each creates a slick that can cover thousands of acres or hundreds of square miles. Floating on the surface, the slick cuts off the sunlight and absorbs the oxygen in the water, smothering the life below. On flowing up to a shore, it coats the birds and animals there, getting into the throats of both and choking them to death, and weighing the birds down so that they cannot fly.

Over the years, several systems have been used to clean away the slicks and have met with varying degrees of success. One method employs a chemical called *elastol*. It turns the slick into a thickish film that can then be pulled off the water with a drumlike machine.

A very popular method calls for the slick to be surrounded by booms so that it cannot escape and then applied with chemicals that break it down into droplets for dispersal by the winds and tides. The first chemicals used were found to be harmful to the surrounding sea life. Less toxic substances have been concocted over the years. Likewise, improved methods of applying them, such as aerial spraying, have been developed.

But there are currently questions about the harms that these less toxic chemicals might be doing to the sea life. And questions as to how to solve some of their shortcomings. As yet, they cannot handle very heavy fuel oil. And their effectiveness is much reduced in exceptionally cold weather.

5

POISONED RIVERS, LAKES, AND WETLANDS

THE WORLD'S RIVERS, LAKES, AND WETLANDS are being damaged by four major factors, one of them being the agricultural activity that has damaged the Aral Sea. Joining it are industry, sewage disposal, and the growth of nearby cities. We begin with what is happening to the planet's rivers.

Filthy Rivers

In *Our Angry Earth*, Isaac Asimov and Frederik Pohl paint a frightening word picture of the poisons in Europe's rivers. They write that 70 percent of Czechoslovakia's waterways are polluted by industrial and human wastes; some

40 percent of the nation's sewage pours directly into the waterways without treatment.

Asimov and Pohl call the great Rhine and Danube rivers "open sewers," choked as they are with industrial, farming, and human wastes. They bluntly say that the Danube "stinks" at points along its run from Germany southeast to Yugoslavia because cities such as Budapest, Hungary, flush their untreated sewage into it, threatening their people with disease-carrying germs and insects, and brewing the dangerous eutrophication that suffocates the surrounding water life.

(It must be noted that the Rhine—which courses through the Netherlands, Germany, and Holland and runs along the French border—is presently the subject of a multinational cleanup program that is returning it to good health.)

As for other rivers, Germany's Elbe is awash with industrial chemicals and an especially dangerous amount of mercury. In the former East Germany, the Saale River is so polluted that the water along half its length cannot be made fit for safe drinking by even the most expensive purification systems.

Other writers have joined Asimov and Pohl in painting bleak pictures of Europe's waterways. A 1995 issue of *Earth Explorer* magazine reported that scientists in the former Soviet Union have been dumping radioactive wastes into many rivers and lakes since the 1950s. The magazine also noted that Soviet industry has polluted many of the country's rivers with such toxins as copper and mercury.

America's Poisoned Rivers

In the United States, the Mississippi River is tainted with industrial wastes, sewage, and agricultural pesticides and fertilizers at many points along its 2,500-mile run from Minnesota to the Gulf of Mexico. The pollution is particularly bad in Louisiana, where intensive oil refining and 25 percent of the nation's chemical manufacturing take place. Dumped into the river along a 150-mile stretch from Baton Rouge to New Orleans is a continual flow of industrial chemicals that include the lethal benzene.

The plant life there has been deeply wounded. The region once produced fine harvests from its pecan trees. They grew to heights of sixty-five to seventy feet. Now, they have shrunk to dwarf size and have lost their limbs.

According to Asimov and Pohl, the people who must drink the river water that seeps into their wells or comes from their taps because they cannot afford bottled water are vulnerable to a wide variety of diseases. They suffer one of the nation's highest death rates from lung, gallbladder, and stomach cancers.

The dangers lurking in the Mississippi can be matched in other American waterways. Consider the Rio Grande. As the river flows along the U.S.-Mexican border on its journey to the Gulf of Mexico, it has been so befouled by the contaminants pouring in from American-owned factories in Mexico and the raw sewage from Mexican border towns—some 60 million tons a day, according to *Earth Explorer*—that a San Antonio newspaper once dubbed it "El Sewer Grande."

Lakes, Pollutants, and Acid Rain

Lakes have suffered pollution as much as rivers. Two of America's Great Lakes—Erie and Michigan—were so polluted in the late 1960s and early 1970s that water officials declared them to be "dead." Swimming was banned at points along their shores. Pregnant women were advised not to eat Lake Michigan fish more than once a week.

Blamed for much of the pollution were the industrial wastes and the urban sewage that flowed in from the cities along the shoreline. Adding to the poisons were the rivers that entered the lakes, one of the most polluted being the Cuyahoga, which reaches Lake Erie at Cleveland. It was so choked with contaminants and sewage that it burst into flames in 1969. Topping off the pollution were the deposits dropped into the Erie and Michigan lakes by commercial shipping.

Fortunately, steps have been taken through the years to cleanse the two lakes. Due in great part to improved sewage disposal methods, pollution is down in the pair and in the Cuyahoga River—though much remains to be done before the cleanup is complete—and they are said to be "alive" again. The authors of the book *Eco-Sanity: A Common-Sense Guide to Environmentalism* (Joseph L. Bast, Peter J. Hill, and Richard C. Rue) report that both lakes are again "fishable and swimmable" and that the Cuyahoga is now "swimmable."

The Cuyahoga fire made headlines throughout the nation when it erupted in 1969. But, since then, another threat to the nation's lakes has been repeatedly mentioned in the press and has become a household term—acid rain.

The Acid Rain Threat

Just as the name indicates, acid rain is precipitation— rain, snow, sleet, and so on—that contains a high acid content. The press has reported that its greatest harm in the United States has been done to the lakes in the nation's eastern and northeastern states.

Though said to do its greatest harm in these states, which range from New York north through New England, it does not originate there. Rather, it comes from the burning of fossil fuels—coal, oil, and natural gas—in states to the west, especially those in the Midwest. When burned in factories, electric power plants, and automobiles, these fuels give off sulfur and nitrogen dioxides that, on rising into the atmosphere, are converted into sulfuric acid and nitric acids by the actions of sunlight and moisture. Then, because most of the United States lies within the latitudinal band in which the prevailing winds come from the west, the acids are borne eastward, finally fanning out to the north and south before returning to earth in rain or some other precipitation.

Acid rain was first noticed at the dawn of the 1970s and was widely reported in the press as wreaking havoc not only in the eastern and northeastern United States but in southeastern Canada as well. It was accused of contaminating some 50,000 lakes in the three regions and killing much of the life in their waters. The next years brought word that the phenomenon was being noted in other areas of the United States, in western Europe, and in Mexico. The affected areas all shared one characteristic in common. Each stood in the path of winds that carried clouds heavily laden with sulfuric acid and nitric acids from regions with fossil-burning factories and power plants. The acid rain was accused not only of damaging lakes but of harming trees and crops as well. There were fears that it also posed a health threat for humans.

The 1970s were marked by a heated debate over the dangers of acid rain, with some scientists saying that it posed a potentially tragic environmental threat, while others felt that concern about its harm was not based on scientific research and that the harm might not be as severe as thought. In 1980, Congress set out to settle the dispute by forming the National Acid Precipitation Assessment Program (NAPAP), a task force that was to study all aspects of the rain and then report on the true extent of its harm. The NAPAP—with a membership of 400 American and Canadian scientists, plus representatives from four research laboratories and twelve government agencies—worked until the dawn of the 1990s before completing its assignment and publishing a report of its findings. Contained in the report were the following points:

> Based on federal government data gathered from 28,300 lakes, the NAPAP claimed that only 3 percent of the total surface area of American lakes was found to be relatively acidic.

Surprisingly, fewer lakes than expected in the hard-hit northeastern states showed themselves to be significantly acidic.

On the other hand, more acidic lakes than expected were found in Florida, where there is less acid rain. Actually, the NAPAP said, half of the surface area of acidic lakes in the United States was located in Florida.

One NAPAP research team went into the Adirondack Mountains to investigate 2,800 lakes said to be devoid of fish due to acid rain. The team found that the rain could be blamed for the absence of fish in only 10 percent of the lakes, saying that other factors were possibly at fault for the absence in the remaining cases.

Just what were those factors? The NAPAP reported that they were the same as those causing a high acid content in other affected lakes, including the Florida lakes. Some were caused by nature and some by human activity.

The natural factors included: the chemistry in the lake waters, the types of vegetation growing on the bottom, the presence of acids due to the sea salts blown into the lakes near the ocean, and the acidity in the soils bordering the lakes. The natural acid content in some lakes was so high that they had either been without fish throughout their history or had lost them to acidity long before acid rain began to make headlines.

The human factors included: the agricultural fertilizers that runoffs carry into the lakes, and the poisons that had entered some lakes when nearby peatlands had been drained for farming. The draining had released a sulfur contained in the peatland soils.

In all, the NAPAP report indicated that acid rain was not the sole cause of lake damage. It was a contributing factor, yes, but there were other factors that did as much or far greater harm. The report added that research had shown that acid rain posed no danger to crops and humans.

The NAPAP report has been widely accepted by scientists, but has been just as widely scorned by environmentalists. The environmentalists argue that some of the task force's findings were invalid because they were based on inadequate research. For example, NAPAP research teams sprayed a variety of food plants—among them wheat and corn—with a simulated acid rain to see what harm would be done. When none was noted by the researchers, the environmentalists charged that "real," not fake, acid rain was needed for the test to have been a valid one.

They also pointed out that the federal government's Environmental Protection Agency (EPA) had issued a report in 1988 that contradicted some of the NAPAP's findings. The EPA reported that streams in the northeast states contained a higher acid content than previously thought.

To this day, the debate continues over whether acid rain is the ecological threat it was thought to be in the 1970s and 1980s. Whatever the truth may be, the federal government has attempted to alleviate the problem by requiring new coal-burning factories and electric power plants to outfit their smokestacks with "scrubbers." These are devices that remove most of the sulfur and nitrogen dioxides from the smoke as it flows up the stacks.

Other measures have been advised for correcting the problem. They include the suggestion that coal with a low sulfur content be burned in the Midwestern factories and power plants. The use of such coal, however, would be an expensive proposition. It would have to be shipped in from a distance because the mines near the factories and plants yield a soft coal with a high sulfur content. The increased expense would raise the cost of Midwestern manufactured goods and electrical power, which, in turn, would raise the price of both for consumers. The same charge has been leveled against the scrubbers, which are costly to install.

Endangered Wetlands

A wetland is defined as an area whose soils contain much moisture. The definition is an accurate but bare-bones one. It gives us, for instance, no indication of the varying sizes of the world's wetlands. It doesn't tell us that they range in size from small water-soaked patches on a farmer's land to swamps, bayous, basins, and deltas that can cover hundreds or thousands of square miles, as does America's Everglades region. Taking shape at the foot of giant Lake Okeechobee in central Florida and fed by the lake waters, the region extends southward through a wide basin for 160 miles to the Gulf of Mexico and encompasses some 4,000 square miles. It is the nation's premier wetland

and is so prized that its southwestern area was set aside as the Everglades National Park in 1947. The park covers some 1.4 million acres.

Nor does the definition of a wetland give us any idea of their nature. There is no mention that they serve as splendid homes for myriad types of wildlife. The home that the Everglades provides is representative on a grand scale of the homes offered by wetlands everywhere. Every year, the Everglades attracts millions of birds, among them ibis, herons, kites, eagles, wood storks, pelicans, and turkey vultures. Prowling its waters are alligators, manatee, cougars, and the Florida panther, which is to be seen nowhere else. As for plants, the area around Lake Okeechobee is decorated with live oak and royal palm trees, and covered with saw grass, whose blades spear twelve feet into the air. To the south are forests of pine, moss-covered cypress, and mangrove trees. The mangroves thrust up majestically to heights of sixty to seventy feet.

Just as the Everglades region can serve as an example of homes made for wildlife by all wetlands, so can it serve as an example of the harm that wetlands throughout the world have endured in our century of multiplying farms, factories, homes, and business buildings.

The Plight of the Everglades

The Everglades took shape some 10,000 years ago when the Ice Age came to an end with the melting of its last great ice sheet. The melting caused the sea level to rise and send water flooding into the low-lying Everglades area, transforming it into a giant river. Yes, river. Most people who visit the region today are surprised to learn that it is not a vast expanse of still water but a 50-mile-wide, shallow river (from a few inches to several feet deep) that moves, constantly and slowly, southward.

Except for the Seminole Indians who lived there and a few assorted pirates and criminals hiding from the law, the Everglades went untouched until the twentieth century. Then decades of work went into the construction of a system of canals and dams that altered the course of much of the Everglades water. Behind the construction projects were two purposes. First, they were intended to supply water for the growing cities nearby, especially Miami. Second, they were meant to drain the water from thousands of acres around Lake Okeechobee and turn them into prime land for dairy, vegetable, and sugarcane farming. Once drained, the acres would be irrigated by the canal water.

The projects did what they were supposed to do—they transformed southern Florida into a highly populated and rich agricultural area. But, at the same time, they created what environmentalists, state and local officials, and thousands of thoughtful citizens came to see as a series of ecological disasters. It was the fears of these people that prompted Congress to establish the Everglades National Park so that construction could never take place there in the future.

The first of the disasters was seen in the region's wildlife. The drainage of the acres around Lake Okeechobee destroyed myriad wildlife habitats. As if the loss of these age-old habitats was not enough, wildlife began to be poisoned by the manures and pesticides that seeped into the southward-moving waters from the new dairies and farms. Just how much harm was done has been estimated by The National Audubon Society—since 1920, a drop of 90 percent in the number of wading birds, among them wood storks and egrets. By themselves, the agricultural pesticides are said to have cut the population of nesting eagles by 70 percent.

The 1970s brought a different problem. Lake Okeechobee suffered an unexpected and dramatic change. Its plants and fish began to die. The killers were the phosphorus and nitrogen in the manures and fertilizers that entered the lake with the runoffs from the surrounding farms. They were triggering the choking process of eutrophication.

Engineers tried to solve the problem by pumping water out of Okeechobee and back to the farmlands. This action did nothing but set the stage for eutrophication to spread to other areas of the Everglades as the water moved southward. The phosphorus and nitrogen in the manures and fertilizers generated new life that took over the waters and destroyed the old. The greatest villain was the cattail plant. It was reported to be spreading through the Everglades and choking off the plant life there at the rate of four acres a day.

Next, Florida's growing number of industries added to the harm—in fact, rounded it off. Into the Everglades went their chemical wastes, with one of the most dangerous being mercury. By the late 1980s, the fish in many areas were being declared unsafe for eating because of the high concentrations of mercury in their systems. For the same reason, a ban was placed on the hunting of alligators for food.

In all, the twentieth century has been a brutal one for the Everglades, with the pollutants spreading so far that they are seeping into the Everglades National Park and causing it to be called the most threatened of America's national parks. But all has not been lost. The government and people of Florida, alarmed at what was happening, began to take steps to correct matters. For one, they put a stop in the early 1990s to the plans for a jetport that would have disturbed the waters of Big Cypress Swamp, which lies just to the north of the Everglades National Park. For another, the U.S. Army Corps of Engineers is embarking on a project to return stretches of the Everglades water to its original course so that it will be restored for its wildlife. For still another, the state of Florida has agreed to a cleanup program that will remove the dangerous chemicals that have invaded the waters.

The U.S. Wetlands: Their Future

Wetlands, both large and small, across the United States have suffered along with the Everglades. Some have lost their wildlife to pollution, as did the Stillwater National Wildlife Refuge in Nevada during the 1980s, when thousands of its fish were killed by toxins that slipped into its waters from surrounding agricultural lands. In the late 1980s, the Fish and Wildlife Service of the Department of the Interior reported that eighty-five animal refuges in all parts of the nation are facing proven, suspected, or potential damages from the agricultural and industrial runoffs into their waters.

American wetlands are both publicly and privately owned. Along with being poisoned, both types have been lost through the years on being drained to provide space for farms, industrial complexes, recreational facilities, suburban neighborhoods, and shopping malls. In all, more than half of the nation's 215 million acres of wetlands have been harmed or destroyed since 1950.

Among the losses were 20 million forested acres along the lower Mississippi River. They were drained some years ago to make way for soybean and other types of farming. But, again, as in the case of the Everglades, all has not been lost. Some of the drained land has proven of little value for agricultural purposes. As a result, approximately 20,000 acres near Vicksburg, Mississippi, are being allowed to return to their original state.

The year 1989 was an important one for the wetlands. It was then that the U.S. government, realizing that the country was sacrificing too many ecologically priceless regions, took steps to reduce future damage. It adopted what it called a "no net loss" policy to safeguard those that it could—those that are federally owned. With certain exceptions, the policy requires that any developer who fills in a federal wetland in one area must create or restore a wetland of equal size in another area.

6

POISONED SEAS—
FROM SEWAGE TO PLASTICS

PEOPLE HAVE USED THE OCEANS as dumping grounds for their refuse for uncounted centuries. It has been the convenient thing to do, and it has seemed the wise thing to do as well. After all, the seas stretch away to the horizons and plunge to spectacular depths. Surely, they have the ability to digest what is cast into them.

In great part, this is true. The oceans do have the power to digest and then cleanse themselves of the pollution that enters them. But they are like humans. Just as we have the ability to absorb certain contaminants (radioactivity, for example) in small amounts, so do the oceans. But we sicken when the dosages become too great for our systems to handle. So do the oceans.

And that is exactly what is happening to them in the twentieth century with the myriad wastes that they must swallow. The pollution has become too great for them to handle. Their tides are coughing up filth on beaches in various parts of the world. The life forms they have long nourished—the fish and mammals and birds—are dying.

At present, the pollution does not seem great in the mid-oceans. It is concentrated in coastal waters, in the shallows of the world's continental shelves. There, the waters have the least chance to disperse the pollution. And there, tragically for every being in the food chain—ourselves included—some 90 percent of all marine creatures live.

The coastal waters are poisoned in the same ways as fresh-water bodies—by the refuse that we pump into them from the shore or that flow in with the runoffs that follow rains and snow. About 90 percent of all the sea pollutants come from the land-based activities.

In addition, the seas—both coastal and deep-water—must endure the refuse cast overboard from all types of ships and pleasure boats; the garbage and sludge (a thick, dark liquid that remains behind when sewage passes through a treatment plant) that are carried miles out from shore aboard barges and dumped; and the oil slicks that result from tanker and drilling rig accidents.

Fortunately, the pollution is not seen along every shore in the world. It is pretty much limited to coasts that have become crowded with cities, industries, and farms in this century. In the 1970s, writer Colin Moorcraft, in his book *Must the Seas Die?*, reported that nine major cities by the sea—among them Japan's Tokyo, America's New York, Brazil's Rio de Janeiro, China's Shanghai, and India's

Bombay—had become home for almost one-fifth of the world's population. It was a percentage that added up to an awesome number of people. And, because more and more people have migrated to the coasts since the 1970s, the number has become even more awesome.

In the United States, the migration has been nothing short of phenomenal. In 1988, *Time* magazine reported that, between 1940 and 1980, the number of Americans living within fifty miles of a seashore had skyrocketed from 42 million to 89 million. The figure is now a quarter-century old. With the continuing growth of the U.S. population (from the 1990 census total of 248.7 million to an estimated 260.8 million in 1995), there can be little doubt that well over 100 million Americans will be living near or alongside the sea when the new century dawns.

How much harm is being inflicted by this migration? Senator John F. Kerry provided part of the answer in 1990 when he reported on the amounts of sewage and industrial wastewaters being poured into American coastal waters each year. Sewage: 2.3 *trillion* gallons. Waste water: 5 *trillion* gallons.

And just what specific harms are being done along America's coasts and all the crowded coasts in the world? Here are some representative examples from recent years.

Polluted Atlantic Shores

In the late 1980s, visitors to the beaches of New York and northern New Jersey were greeted with a nauseating surprise. For years, the beaches and their waters had been clean and inviting to swimmers and picnickers. But now, suddenly, the Atlantic was befouling them with a host of sickening wastes. Floating in the surf and sweeping up to the sands were blobs of sewage, plastic debris, drug paraphernalia that included needles and syringes, and medical refuse that ranged from prescription bottles and blood-stained bandages to vials of blood. Some of the medical wastes were radioactive.

The ugly onslaught resulted in fifty miles of New York beaches being closed to swimming for months. In New Jersey, the income earned from tourism fell almost to nothing as people shunned not only the stained northern beaches but also those 100 or more miles to the south that had gone untouched. Many businesses were threatened with failure. Thousands of workers faced the possibility of lost jobs.

The press reported that the filth came from a combination of sources—from wastes being pumped into the Atlantic from New York City, from tons of sludge that had been towed more than 100 miles out to sea on barges and dumped, and from a sewage treatment plant at New Jersey's Asbury Park. Because of an accident, the plant had spilled millions of gallons of raw sewage into the sea.

Rather than being dispersed by the waters, all the filth had been caught for a time in the to-and-fro action of the tides and had been washed ashore.

Governors Thomas H. Kean of New Jersey and Mario Cuomo of New York immediately took action against the sludge and the toxic medical wastes. Both declared that the dumping of sludge off their coasts must end by 1991. They then called for the development of regulations that would require a "cradle-to-grave" tracking of the wastes from their inception to their disposal. Records would be kept of the places where they were created, of the methods used to transport them to their disposal sites, and of the sites themselves. Any facility that violated the regulations would be prosecuted and fined.

The Minamata Bay Tragedy

In the early 1950s, the people who lived along the shores of Minamata Bay on Japan's Kyushu Island began to fall prey to a mysterious illness. It was marked by a growing numbness in their faces and limbs and was often accompanied by convulsions, speech difficulties, and the partial loss of vision. In a three-year period, while bewildered doctors tried to identify the illness, it struck more than 200 people and claimed fifty-three lives. Several women victims gave birth to mentally and physically damaged children.

In those three years, the doctors thought that any of several illnesses might be at work, among them meningitis (an inflammation of the membranes that envelop the brain and spinal cord), brain tumors, and encephalitis (an inflammation of the brain). In the end, however, the villain proved to be mercury.

For some twenty years, a plastics plant had been disgorging the heavy metal into a nearby river. It had flowed down the river and into Minamata Bay, where it had slowly worked its way up the food chain there, building to toxic levels first in tiny crustaceans and, finally, in the bay's large fish. Once the fish were poisoned, they began to poison the people for whom they were a daily staple.

The Minamata tragedy is important in the history of marine pollution. It stands as one of the earliest incidents to warn that the seas and the life in them are vulnerable to injury when fed too much of the modern world's pollution and that the injury can reach out to touch humans.

Sea Life At Risk

In the years since the Minamata Bay fish were poisoned, reports of sea life sickened and killed by pollutants have arrived from all the world's oceans.

One report came to light in 1983 when high levels of radioactivity were discovered in the Irish Sea, just off the coast of northwest England. At fault was coolant water leaking from a pipeline belonging to the nuclear power plant at Sellafield. Poisoned mussels were found for miles along the beaches stretching away from the plant. In her book, *Mother Country*, Marilynne Robinson reports that, thanks to the Sellafield plant, the fish in the Irish Sea are 5,000 times more radioactive than those in the North Sea, which lies on the far side of England and has also been contaminated with radioactivity.

In 1985, a Greek freighter ran aground in the harbor at Mogadishu, Somalia, on Africa's northeastern coast alongside the Indian Ocean. Spilled into the waters was much of the ship's cargo of toxic pesticides, solvents, and lead compounds. The spill poisoned the life in the harbor waters and forced 300,000 townspeople to flee their homes for several weeks.

Though, as these incidents show, the harm done in foreign seas has been bad, the death toll in U.S. coastal waters from poisoning has stood second to none in recent years. In 1988, at least 750 dolphins died mysteriously in the Atlantic and began washing ashore. Their carcasses were terrible to see. Many had lost great patches of skin; the patches had not been bitten away by predators but had crumbled and fallen off. Others had snouts, tails, and fins that were covered with blisters and holes. When some of the corpses were examined, they were found to contain exceptionally high levels of PCBs. One victim's body was riddled with 6,800 parts per million of PCBs. The federal government sets a maximum of a scant two parts per million in fish considered safe for eating.

Deadly Plastics

Joining toxic substances as terrible dangers to sea life are today's myriad plastic products. Ranging from miles-long fishing nets to sandwich bags, picnic plates, and styrofoam cups, they do not kill by poisoning. Rather, they kill by choking or starving their victims to death.

Responsible for many deaths are the nets that break

away from fishing boats. They are strong and lightweight and can stretch for miles. Into them blunder fish, mammals, dolphins, and seals, there to remain trapped until they die of starvation. Several years ago, a group of environmentalists came upon a drifting net in Alaskan waters. It measured twenty miles long and, when they pulled it from the sea, they found that it had snared and taken the lives of hundreds of salmon and 350 birds.

While the nets are a great danger, individual plastic wares constitute an even greater threat. Take plastic fishing line, for example. A turtle died in New York waters after swallowing 590 yards of the line.

Or consider those soft drink and beer six-pack rings. Fish swim up to them, poke their noses through any of the openings, and, unable to escape, die of starvation.

Or think of those innocent-looking sandwich bags. Sea turtles mistake them for jellyfish and attempt to eat them, only to be doomed when the bags block their stomachs and intestines and make further eating impossible.

The turtles are not attracted to the bags alone. When the stomach of a dead turtle that had washed ashore in Hawaii was examined, it was found to contain not only several bags but also a comb, a plastic flower, dozens of bits of plastic, and a plastic golf tee. The turtle weighed twelve pounds, with the plastic items accounting for two of those pounds.

It is estimated that plastic wastes have killed as many as 2 million seabirds and 100,000 fish and other creatures each year. One estimate holds that 50,000 young fur seals lose their lives annually when they become trapped in fishing nets.

The death toll is not surprising when we consider the amounts of plastic materials that have been deposited in the sea over the years. Marine biologist Sylvia Earle, in her book *Sea Change: A Message of the Oceans*, writes that a 1975 study by the National Academy of Sciences found that 14 billion pounds of garbage, much of it plastic in nature, was being dumped into the seas every year from merchant and passenger ships, fishing boats, pleasure craft, tankers, offshore drilling rigs, and other sources.

Moving forward little more than a decade, she cites a report from the Center for Marine Conservation (CMC) which pointed out that, prior to 1988, the world's merchant ships dumped at least 450,000 plastic items into the sea every day (plus 300,000 glass and 4.8 million metal containers). The CMC, founded in 1972 and headquartered in Washington, D.C., works to protect marine wildlife, coastlines, and ocean resources. Since the mid-1980s, it has spearheaded an annual cleanup of the nation's beaches. Each year, the program attracts thousands of volunteer workers to all of America's coastlines.

The plastic waste problem became so great in U.S. coastal waters that Congress took action to correct it in 1987 with the Marine Plastic Pollution Control Act. (It is because of the Act that the above CMC report covers only plastic dumpings prior to 1988.) It was, as we'll see later, one of several major Congressional measures enacted between the 1960s and 1990 to control not only the disposal of plastics at sea but the dumping of garbage and other pollutants as well.

Despite these laws, the ocean dumping of pollutants continues to be a problem. Another type of contamination, however, captures headlines throughout the world today when it is at its worst.

7

POISONED SEAS—
OIL SPILLS

As you know, thousands of oil spills, some accidental and some deliberate, occur annually in the world's oceans. It is estimated that between 10,000 and 16,000 take place each year in U.S. waters alone.

Most spills go unreported by the press because they affect only small areas and are quickly dispersed by the sea. But the same cannot be said of the most serious of spills. Resulting from tanker and offshore drilling rig accidents, they are reported in the news worldwide because they spread black slicks over vast expanses—sometimes hundreds, even thousands, of square miles—and inflict great harm to the shores within their reach.

These spills have been especially great in the last forty years. This is due to the fact that the size of tankers and offshore drilling rigs has steadily increased during those years. In the late 1940s, the largest tankers weighed no more than 26,000 deadweight tons. But, by the early 1970s, the oceans were being sailed by tankers weighing 200,000 deadweight tons and carrying ten times the cargoes earlier hauled by tankers. Today, there are goliaths that measure the length of several football fields and weigh in at 500,000 deadweight tons.

As for the drilling rigs, the first of their number was constructed off the southern California coast in 1895. It consisted of nothing more than a small wooden platform and a squat wooden derrick. Today's rigs, pumping thousands of barrels a day (with forty-two gallons to the barrel), tower hundreds of feet into the air, stand on concrete piles embedded in the seafloor, feature massive platforms and derricks, and provide offices, workshops, laboratories, and living accommodations for workers.

Just how large have the spills been in recent years? Here are some of the greatest that have resulted from tanker accidents.

1967:   The *Torrey Canyon* goes aground a few miles off Land's End at the southwestern tip of England, spilling 119,000 tons—an estimated 35 million gallons—of crude oil into the Atlantic. The spill continues for days and is finally stopped when British fliers set the ship and the surrounding slick afire with napalm bombs.

1969:   The earliest major spill in U.S. waters takes place when the hull of the *Keo* gives out and breaks open. Emptied into the waters off Massachusetts are 8 million gallons of oil.

1976: The Massachusetts waters are again befouled, this time when the *Argo Merchant* grinds to a halt on the Nantucket shoals and releases 7.7 million gallons of dense fuel oil.

1978: The *Amoco Cadiz* runs aground a little more than a mile off the French coast after its steering gear malfunctions. Over 60 million gallons flow from the ship's ruptured hull. The stricken vessel continues disgorging oil for eleven days before aerial bombings put an end to its agony. An estimated 80,000 gallons wash ashore, befoul the beaches and wildlife, and cause headaches and nausea among the people living there.

1979: The first of the two largest spills in American waters is recorded this year. It occurs when a collision in Galveston Bay, Texas, tears a hole in the *Burmah Agate*. Into the bay pour about 11 million gallons.

1989: This year marks the second of the two greatest American spills. The tanker *Exxon Valdez* runs aground while sailing in Alaska's Prince William Sound. It, too, empties some 11 million gallons into the sea.

And what of the biggest drilling rig spills? One of the worst to stain American waters occurred in 1969. In February, a rig owned by the Union Oil Company blew out of control in California's Santa Barbara Channel. Weeks were to pass before the well was successfully capped. In that time, the well loosed up to 21,000 gallons of oil a day and created a slick that spread out over 540 square miles in the Pacific.

The worst drilling rig spill in the western hemisphere occurred in 1979 when another rig blew out of control, this one in the Ixtoc field off the eastern coast of Mexico. The well ran wild for nine months and spewed 600,000 tons of crude oil into the Gulf of Mexico—a total of more than 170 million gallons.

The damage done by the rampaging Ixtoc well was approximated far across the world twelve years later—but not as the result of an accident. In 1991, during the Persian Gulf War, Iraq's Saddam Hussein opened the valves at Kuwait's Sea Island Terminal and began dumping tons of oil into the Gulf. The reasons for this action were unclear—and remain unclear to this day. Perhaps Saddam was trying to hamper the U.S. warships that were blockading the Gulf; perhaps he hoped to cripple the desalination plant that was converting salt water into fresh water for Saudi Arabia. Whatever the case, a black slick spread out into the Gulf, but was soon stopped when U.S. planes bombed the terminal and closed off its pipes. Estimates vary on the amount of oil that escaped into the Gulf. They range from a low of 25 million gallons to a high of 130 million.

An Oil Controversy

There is little doubt that oil spills, blackening great stretches of the water and the nearby beaches as they do, are the most visible of all sea contaminations. But there is disagreement over how much harm they actually do and how long they continue to damage the sea and the life in it. Some environmental groups contend that they do long-term harm, arguing that their damages persist for years. Other experts in the subject claim that the damage, while severe, is short-lived.

The environmental groups argue that, as a slick breaks up, it becomes myriad droplets that descend to the ocean floor. On mingling with the sediment there, they can then remain in place for years, centuries, or beyond, killing the surrounding flora and fauna. In time, the area is bereft of all life, except for species that are capable of surviving in a poisoned habitat.

On the opposite side of the argument are those who contend that the sea, with its ability to disperse poisons and cleanse itself, makes relatively short work of spills. Authors Joseph L. Bast, Peter J. Hill, and Richard C. Rue report on this view in their book *Eco-Sanity: A Common-Sense Guide to Envionmentalism* when they write of how scientists found that Alaska's Prince William Sound was healing itself after the *Exxon Valdez's* spill in 1989.

They describe what the scientists learned about the Sound's seafloor and waters while observing the massive cleanup funded and conducted by the Exxon Corporation. To begin, the scientists found that the seafloor showed no signs of the *Exxon Valdez* oil whatsoever. What remained of the ship's oil was confined to small bays near the shore.

At the same time, they found that most of the oil in the Sound had been put there over a long period of years by nature and not man-made sources. It had seeped into the waters through cracks in geologic formations outside Prince William Sound.

Finally, the scientists noted that, in addition to the oil naturally in the Sound, there was oil from small spills— from boating operations, leaking fuel tanks, and various onshore activities—that had accumulated through decades and posed a potential problem for the waters.

But, since virtually all the spilled *Exxon Valdez* oil had disappeared, a question had to be asked. Where did it go? The authors reply that the ocean's circulation took care of part of the problem; it replaces the waters in the Sound every twenty days. Also at work was evaporation; within the first forty-eight hours after a spill, some 40 percent of spilled oil evaporates; from then on it continues to evaporate at a slower rate. Finally, to top things off, between 90 and 95 percent of the oil that remains behind is broken down and eaten by bacteria and other life forms in the water.

As for the fish in the Sound, the three authors cite a report that its herring and salmon were soon thriving again. The greatest harm, the authors contend, was done to the shores blackened with the oil. Seemingly countless marine species—algae, crabs, mollusks, and birds—had been sickened, with death being the fate of thousands.

But the shores themselves had shown a remarkable ability for self-healing. In fact, the beaches that had *not* been visited by volunteer cleanup crews had recovered more quickly than those tended by the crews.

Sylvia Earle, as she writes in *Sea Change: A Message of the Oceans*, came to the same conclusion when visiting the Sound. She believes that, at the same time that the shoreline cleanup was doing spectacular good, the booted feet of the volunteer crews and the hot water used for the cleansing work were doing an unintentional harm. They were trampling and burning much of the life that had survived the spill and that they were trying to help.

In all, the authors of *Eco-Sanity* say that the findings of the scientists who watched the cleanup of Prince William Sound do *not* prove that the spills fail to cause short-term and—especially for the surrounding sea life—tragic damage. But they do strongly demonstrate that the damage is not as long-lasting as many environmental groups believe.

Environmentalists, however, challenge many of these findings. In 1996, seven years after the *Exxon Valdez* accident, they claimed that the Sound was yet showing signs of damage. At midyear, ten afflicted beaches were still scarred with blobs of oil and were due to be cleaned, at a cost of $2 million (from the Exxon Corporation).

Further, the environmentalists pointed out that the animals and birds in Prince William Sound were still suffering. The numbers of seals, harlequin ducks, and several species of seabirds had declined after the spill and were continuing to do so. The environmentalists admitted that the seals in the region were in decline prior to the spill, but added that the continuing decline was greater in the spill area than elsewhere.

This has prompted the question: Did the spill affect the seals' food supply in ways that have yet to be discovered? The same question is being asked about the Pacific herring that inhabit Alaska's coast. Their numbers suddenly began to fall in 1993, four years after the spill. Did the stress of the accident on their lives make them more susceptible to killer diseases? Research is currently seeking out the answers to these questions.

Thus far, with most reports of damage coming from coastal waters, it seems as if the mid-ocean depths have managed to digest and cleanse themselves of the wastes that have been cast into them. But we must not become complacent about their health. When, in 1951, the Norwegian anthropologist and explorer Thor Heyerdahl sailed his papyrus raft *Kon Tiki* across the Atlantic from Africa to South America, he announced that he had sighted not one trace of man-made pollution. But when he traveled the same waters again—this time in 1972—he sighted globs of oil on forty of the fifty-seven days needed to complete the voyage. By then, the ocean depths were under attack. Are they under greater attack today, a siege that, waged beneath the waves, we cannot yet see?

8

THE BATTLE FOR CLEAN WATER

THOUGH WATER POLLUTION has plagued the world in our century, it has not been allowed to reign unchecked. It has been fought everywhere by governments, organizations, and dedicated individuals.

International Actions

The international actions have all dealt with safeguarding the oceans and have taken the form of multination treaties, with the earliest of their number targeted at oil pollution. The first major treaty was signed in 1954 and was called the International Convention for the Prevention of the Pollution of the Sea by Oil. Known popularly as OILPOL, it was aimed against the deliberate dumping of oil wastes into the oceans when ships were emptying their bilges. The signatory countries pledged that their ships would end the practice and would wait until they reached ports where the wastes could be emptied into tanks ashore. The nations were to provide such tanks for the ships that visited their ports regularly.

Amendments were added to the pact in 1962. They included the call for the signatory countries to study possible methods for confining spills and removing them from the sea.

In 1972, OILPOL was joined by a far more extensive pact—the Convention on the Prevention of Marine Pollution by Dumping of Wastes and Other Matter. Signed by sixty-one countries, it was not limited to oil pollution but called for the signatory nations to develop measures that would protect the oceans against a wide variety of contaminants. The materials that could no longer be dumped included hydrocarbons, mercury and mercury compounds, and radioactive materials.

The most significant of all the international pacts came a year later, in 1973, with the signing of the International Convention for the Prevention of Pollution from Ships. Known popularly as MARPOL (combined abbreviations of the terms *marine* and *pollution*), it went beyond calling for the signatory nations to develop antipollution measures. Rather, it established regulations to control the dumping of sewage and noxious liquids and solids. In addition, it contained regulations against land dumpings that would eventually work their way into the sea.

Further, MARPOL, made the disposal of garbage by

ships illegal within certain distances from the shore and established penalties of $25,000 to $50,000 for each illegal dumping, plus possible imprisonment of up to five years for the offender. The distances were established on the basis of the sea's ability to digest the types of garbage and the dangers that they each posed for marine life. The growing number of plastic wastes that the years had brought were recognized as particularly dangerous. MARPOL dictated that ships may not dump:

Plastic items and garbage consisting of paper, rags, metal, glass, crockery, dunnage (packing materials and linings that float), and food when sailing *within three miles from shore*.

Plastic items, dunnage, and garbage consisting of paper, rages, metal, glass, crockery, and food when between *three and twelve miles offshore*.

Plastic items and dunnage when *twelve to twenty-five miles out to sea*.

Plastic items when *beyond twenty-five miles from shore*.

The United States was among the countries that signed the MARPOL pact. In 1987, when plastic wastes were doing so much to befoul the nation's coastal waters, Congress strengthened the nation's position against them by passing the Marine Plastic Pollution Control Act. The Act went beyond outlawing the dumping of plastics offshore;

it banned the practice in the country's rivers, lakes, bays, and sounds as well. Further, the measure prohibited the dumping of plastics at sea by all American ships and the disposal of plastic wastes in U.S. waters out to a distance of 200 miles from the nation's coastlines.

The decades have brought a number of other global pacts. They include: the International Convention on Civil Liability for Oil Pollution Damage (1969), which was enacted in the wake of the *Torrey Canyon's* 35 million-gallon spill in 1967 and established the framework by which harmed countries and other parties can recover the costs for spill damages and cleanup operations; the Convention for the Prevention of Marine Pollution from Land-based Sources (1974); and the Declaration for the Protection of the Arctic Environment (1991).

The treaties have been helpful, but they have all suffered a shortcoming. They depend on the integrity of ships' captains to make them work. Unfortunately, especially when sailing outside territorial waters, many captains continue to dump their oil wastes and other debris in the sea. Remember Thor Heyerdahl's experience on the *Kon Tiki's* second voyage across the Atlantic from Africa to South America.

National Actions: Coastal Waters

America's first antipollution measures were aimed at protecting its coastal waters. The first of their number took shape more than a century ago, in the late 1880s when New York City was experiencing a building boom. So much construction rubbish was being dumped into the city's harbor that Congress made it illegal for the practice to continue. The ban not only covered the harbor itself but also the tributaries flowing into it, plus the reaches of Long Island Sound. Then, at the close of the century, Congress extended the ban to all U.S. navigable waterways, doing so with the passage of the Rivers and Harbor Act.

The next major United States legislation came in 1924. Congress that year enacted the Oil Pollution Act. It prohibited tankers and ships powered by oil fuel from discharging oil into the country's territorial waters, which extended three miles from shore.

The Act stands as the first U.S. law to control marine oil pollution and was followed thirty-seven years later by the Oil Pollution Act of 1961. This new legislation stemmed from the nation's signing of the OILPOL pact. It outlawed the discharge of oil into coastal zones and fisheries throughout the world.

As was true on the international scene, a number of national measures were passed in the next years to control ocean pollution. One of the most significant was the Ocean Dumping Act of 1972, which banned the disposal of an assortment of dangerous materials into U.S. territorial waters. The materials included high-level radioactive wastes, heavy metals (among them cadmium and mercury), and substances used for the manufacture of weapons for chemical and biological warfare.

The 1980s brought several more measures, one of which was the already described 1987 Marine Plastic Pollution Control Act. In the years since its passage, many people have wondered if the Act has actually been doing any good because plastic wastes continue to roll up on the country's shores from the sea and continue to kill myriad sea creatures.

Especially concerned are the volunteers who participate in the annual cleanups of the nation's beaches spearheaded by the Washington, D.C.-based Center for Marine Conservation. Each year they've found tons of plastic wastes in the sands, divided between junk left there by careless visitors and debris that has floated in from the sea. In the 1989 cleanup, for instance, the volunteers who were working a 300-mile stretch of Texas coastline retrieved more than 15,600 six-pack rings. The 140,000 volunteers who moved along 3,000 beaches in the 1995 cleanup reported that plastic discards made up the greatest percentage of the trash collected—59 percent, with glass, paper, metal, wood, cloth, and rubber all trailing behind.

But the volunteers sounded a positive note at the end of the 1995 cleanup. They said that, while the number of plastic items that could be identified as coming from the sea was still great, it was not as great as in years past. It was now exceeded by the amount of plastic items left on the beaches by visitors.

The note was indeed a positive one. But there is still plastic trash rolling in from the sea. Like many tankers with their oil wastes, some ships and pleasure boats continue to dump their trash overboard. One cruise ship was recently caught dumping and its owner was fined $500,000.

While the Marine Plastic Pollution Control Act was the congressional response to a general problem, another measure was a reply to a specific incident—the 1989 *Exxon Valdez* oil spill of 11 million gallons in Alaska's Prince William Sound. It led to the passage of the Oil Pollution Act of 1990. The Act contains a series of stringent provisions directed at reducing the spills. Here are three representative examples:

The financial liability (the amount that the owners could be forced to pay for damages and cleanup operations) for medium-sized supertankers suffering a spill in U.S. waters is set at approximately $100 million. Under earlier U.S. regulations, the liability had been approximately $14 million.

The liability for a spill that occurs while a tanker captain is intoxicated is set at an unlimited amount. (At the time of the *Exxon Valdez* accident, the tanker's captain was alleged to have been intoxicated.)

All new tankers sailing in American waters are required to have double hulls. Single-hull tankers are to be refitted with double hulls over a period of years, with all single-hull vessels to be phased out by the year 2010.

National Actions: Fresh Waters

While the earliest national water measures were directed against polluting the seas, it was not until the late 1960s, when Ohio's chemically befouled Cuyahoga River burst into flames and other problems were making headlines that Congress began tackling legislation to protect the nation's fresh waters.

The nation's first major fresh-water legislation was the Federal Water Pollution Control Act of 1972. In the Act and again in its 1977 amendments, Congress set two major goals for America's fresh waters. First, they were to be made fit for the life in them and for fishing, swimming, and other water activities by 1983. Second, the discharge of pollutants into the country's navigable waterways was to be eliminated by 1985.

In addition, the Act and its 1977 amendments stipulated that the federal government, in cooperation with the states, water authorities, and concerned organizations, would promote and provide funds for research programs aimed at ending the discharge of pollutants not only into the country's navigable waterways but its coastal waters as well. Federal grants would also be available for the construction of new sewage treatment plants.

Finally, Congress ordered the government's Environmental Protection Agency (EPA) to administer the Act and then develop a set of strict standards for the discharge of sewage into the country's waters.

The Act did substantial good, but many cities and regions, in the limited time given until the 1983 and 1985 goals came due, were unable to meet them. As a result, Congress passed a new measure—the Clean Water Act—in 1987. As did its predecessor, the new act provided funding for the construction of treatment plants. It also called for the cleansing of befouled estuaries, toxic waters, and polluted industrial and agricultural runoffs.

In the years since the enactment of the Federal Water Pollution Control Act of 1972, billions of dollars have been spent by the federal government, private industry, and municipalities to comply with the regulations set forward in the measure and its amendments. During the 1980s alone, some $23 billion were spent each year. Since 1972, more than $75 billion in tax funds have gone into the construction of municipal treatment plants, with the government providing up to 75 percent of the money needed to build them.

Because of these antipollution measures—and steps taken by the states and private industries—the quality of the nation's fresh water in the 1990s is said to be better than ever before. But there is still much room for improvement. The United States continues to house many aging treatment plants and water systems in need of upgrading or replacement, a problem that the 1996 Safe Drinking Water Act (see Chapter 4) is attempting to solve with additional federal funds for new construction.

Though the 1972 and 1987 Acts have been successful, they have also run into criticism. One criticism is pointed out in the book *Eco-Sanity: A Common-Sense Guide to Environmentalism.* Its authors remark that not all the money provided by the two measures has been spent efficiently. The high technological standards set by the EPA for treatment plant construction have often meant that cities and regions could not pursue less expensive but just as effective ways to handle their sewage. Further, the accent has been on building treatment plants and has caused the nation to overlook ways to reduce the runoffs from farms, factories, construction sites, and watered lawns. Those runoffs, the authors claim, are responsible for 57 to 98 percent of the pollutants entering the nation's lakes and rivers.

The book also points out that, after years of heavy polluting by industry, agriculture, and cities, the quality of the country's waters was beginning to improve in the 1960s due to state, industrial, and agricultural efforts, well before the Federal Water Pollution Control Act of 1972 came into being. The quality has continued to improve through the years with the help of it and the Clean Water Act. The improvement has been slow in some areas but dramatic in others—for example, the improved conditions in the once-flaming Cuyahoga River and in two of the Great Lakes, Erie and Michigan.

States and Local Areas

States and local areas have enacted laws to conserve and protect their fresh-water supplies. To the laws they've added a variety of conservation and protection strategies.

One widely used strategy calls for the recycling of the wastewater in sewage treatment plants so that it can be made to do a number of jobs that would otherwise require the use of fresh water. The wastewater, which is called reclaimed water, must be purified to the point where it is so free of disease-causing substances that it will pose no health hazards. Factories today employ reclaimed water in their manufacturing processes; cities wash down their streets and water their parks and playgrounds with it; and farmers use it to irrigate their crops. Current studies show that, if treated sufficiently, wastewater is fit for drinking.

Other recyclings are meant in great part to keep such refuse as oil, paper, plastics, glass, and metal from entering the local water systems. For example, when a car's oil is being changed, a growing number of cities today either discourage or prohibit the old practice of letting the used oils flow away into a drainage system. They are now drained into cans and then taken to a recycling center for disposal or placed in special containers at curbside for pickup by the local garbage service. Along with safeguarding the water, the recycling enables the materials to be used again and thus conserves the natural resources that made them possible. Oil is recycled for use as industrial fuel; recycled paper is not only used again as paper but also goes into the manufacture of building insulation and plasterboard.

One of the most ambitious recycling programs in the country has been seen in California and was undertaken as a water conservation effort. During a lengthy period of drought in the 1980s, California's industries decided that, if they hoped to have a continuing supply of water for their manufacturing processes, they had to save the amount they already had on hand by recycling it for further use. To get the job done, they installed new equipment in their factories and altered some of their traditional production methods. The results of their work were phenomenal, as was evident in a 1990–91 survey of 640 manufacturing plants in twelve counties. The survey revealed that the plants had saved more than 331.9 million cubic feet of water in 1989 alone, as compared to the amount used in 1985. The saving equaled the yearly water consumption of 150,000 homes. The recycling-conservation program not only saw the industries through the drought of the 1980s but set them up to take future droughts in stride.

California is not the only state to have witnessed a major conservation effort. At the opposite end of the country, the greater metropolitan area of Boston, Massachusetts, was faced in the 1980s with the possibility of having to construct a costly water project that would tap distant rivers to meet the needs of its growing population. However, in response to advice from environmental groups that the river waters would taint Boston's supply, the city's water district elected to try a massive water conservation program instead. The program was launched in 1987 and involved several individual campaigns. Water-saving devices were placed in approximately 100,000 homes. Leaking pipes were found and repaired. Several hundred businesses were coached in water-saving strategies. More than a million water conversation booklets, pamphlets, and other publications were distributed to thousands of schoolchildren. The result: between 1987 and 1991, the yearly demand for water by the district's 2.5 million customers dropped from 1.6 billion cubic feet to 1.3 billion. (Despite the savings realized by the program, Boston may yet have to expand its water system to meet its needs.)

The years of drought that drove California's industries to action were endured in various parts of the United States. They gave birth to conservation measures that are now being continued in many areas as routine methods for harboring the local water supplies. Families in those areas are still being urged to employ such tactics as cutting their shower times in half, turning off their hoses when washing their cars down with soap and saving the hoses for rinsing only, installing devices to lessen the water when toilets are flushed, and reducing the time taken to water lawns.

Lawns, which require a great deal of water to thrive, are a particular enemy of dry regions. While many areas are pleading that less water be used on them, at least one city—Tucson, Arizona—has taken definite action. In 1991, the city fathers approved a regulation that prohibits new housing developments from devoting more than 10 percent of their landscaping to lawns.

A new and interesting anti-lawn approach is being encouraged in several states and may soon spread to others. It encourages the use of what are known as Xeriscape plants to reduce the area of home, park, and highway median strip lawns. The plants, with their name coming from the Greek word *xeros* (meaning *dry*) can flourish with far less water than is required for grass—some 30 to 80 percent less. In one western city, a study showed that their use cut the amount of water for gardening by some 54 percent.

Another interesting approach that is meeting with success is called water trading. The way it works can be seen in California, where the city of Los Angeles recently spent $230 million dollars to modernize the irrigation system for surrounding farms. In trade for the system, the farmers gave the city their rights to use the water that they do not need or that would otherwise be wasted.

In still another approach, California and Florida are turning to desalination plants, which convert seawater into fresh water. Florida's coastline is already dotted with some 100 small desalination units. The largest desalination plant in the United States (capable of producing over 89,000 cubic feet of water daily) is located at Santa Barbara, California, and the state has been planning to install others all along its length.

In all, there are presently more than 7,500 desalination plants in the world. Among the countries they serve in addition to the United States are Australia, Greece, Kuwait, Israel, Italy, Russia, and Saudi Arabia.

Desalination has a major drawback that has kept more countries from employing it. The cost of converting the seawater to fresh water is high. Consequently, when that cost is passed on to consumers, they must pay several times the average price of water obtained from regular water systems—usually between four and eight times in the United States. Because the costs of their water are so great to users and because they are expensive to construct, desalination plants account for just one-tenth of 1 percent of the world's total fresh-water use.

That figure may one day rise, however, due to a number of possible factors. Some nations may be forced to desalination when their increasing industrial production puts too severe a strain on their local fresh-water supplies; some when they see that lands now arid can be made fit for farming with desalination; and when some, especially in the water-poor Middle East and Africa, deplete their fresh-water supplies to the point where they must turn to desalination for survival.

Unfortunately, water conservation programs are today pretty well limited to the advanced countries and are going ignored in most third-world nations. Hopefully, this is a situation that will change in the future. In the meantime, we in the United States can feel fortunate. Our people are concerned about water purity and conservation. The country is blessed with a rich supply of fresh water. And we have the financial ability to meet the costs that water protection and conservation programs entail.

9

CAN YOU BE
OF HELP?

THE PROBLEMS BESETTING the world's fresh and salt waters are so many and so wide-ranging that you may feel you can do little or nothing to solve them. This is a very understandable feeling that is shared by many, but it's also a mistaken one. Remember that efforts are being made worldwide to improve matters. There are many things that you, as a young person now and as an adult later, can do to help.

Let's start with some steps that you can take right away, this very day.

Learn Everything You Can

I hope this book has provided you with much valuable information about water pollution. But, if you plan to be of any real help, you must not depend on just one book to give you all the information you need. No single book can tell you all there is to know about an ongoing problem. The problem will always stay ahead of you because it will be constantly changing. New facts will come to light. There will be incidents, political developments, and technological advances that will either help to solve the problem or worsen it. Continuing study is needed to stay abreast of everything that is happening.

To begin gathering more information about our poisoned waters, check the books listed in the bibliography at the end of this book. They are all written by experts in environmental matters and are available at most public libraries.

Though they all contain solid information, I'm going to highlight three of them that I have found to be especially valuable.

Last Oasis: Facing Water Scarcity by Sandra Postel. Sandra Postel is vice-president for research at Worldwatch Institute. The book is limited to just one problem—the overuse that is depleting the world's supply of fresh water—but it is "must" reading because of the seriousness of the subject. The book not only describes the problem but also discusses technologies and methods that can be employed to ease it.

Eco-Sanity: A Common-Sense Guide to Environmentalism by Joseph L. Bast, Peter J. Hill, and Richard C. Rue covers various environmental problems, but gives a fair share of space to water pollution. The book is particularly interesting in that it speaks out against the "scare" tactics that some environmental groups and individuals employ when alerting the public to an ecological threat. They use the tactics to strengthen their message—often making the problem look worse than it actually is—and to raise the funds necessary for their work. The authors themselves are environmentalists.

Sea Change: A Message of the Oceans by Sylvia Earle. Sylvia Earle is a marine biologist and the former chief scientist of the National Oceanographic and Atmospheric Association. In 1981, she founded Deep Ocean Engineering, a company that builds deep submersibles, and now serves as its director. *Sea Change* is beautifully written, contains many facts concerning the ocean depths that she has explored, and reads like an adventure story.

While books will add much to your knowledge, you should not limit your reading to them. To keep abreast of the newest threats to our waters and the latest developments meant to help improve matters, you need to turn to the media. Newspapers, magazines, and radio and television newscasts and documentaries should be constantly checked.

Also, don't limit your studies to water pollution alone. The atmosphere and the land are being stained by pollution as much as the water. Learn what is happening to them. The problems of all three are intertwined. For example, the massive deforestation that is occurring in parts of the world to make way for factories, farms, cities, and tourist recreational facilities is not only disturbing local wind and rain patterns and the ecology of the surrounding lands but the nearby waters as well. The removal of the tree roots loosens the soil, which is then carried into the waters in greater amounts than before by runoffs. It brings with it nutrients that generate the deadly eutrophication.

By learning how the various environmental problems are linked, you'll add immeasurably to your understanding of the water problem.

A Balanced Point of View

For as long as you are learning about water pollution, or any subject, you'll be wise to adopt a certain attitude—a balanced point of view. You're going to read and hear many conflicting claims about water pollution and you must take care to keep yourself from immediately jumping in and agreeing or disagreeing with any of them. You're going to have to give some time and thought to deciding which to believe.

Suppose that you read two magazine articles. One tells you that a certain water pollutant will harm you, while the other maintains that it's about as dangerous as a hangnail. Which one are you to believe? With a balanced point of view, you'll begin looking for the answer by rereading the articles to see which writer has presented research that strikes you as being more solid than the other.

Then you'll move on to find out what other experts in the field are saying. Only after you've gathered enough solid evidence to feel certain one way or the other will it be time to make a final decision. Don't be hasty in arriving at your own point of view.

One special point: from time to time, you'll come across books that tell you that an ecological problem will lead to worldwide disaster in the near future. These are called "doomsday" books. One of their number, *The Population Bomb* by Paul Ehrlich, was published in the late 1960s and predicted global famines and the death of hundreds of millions of people in the 1970s because of the rapid multiplication of the planet's population. Such books make frightening reading, but don't swallow them whole. Consider what they have to say—they often contain some valid information—but always remember one thing: dire predictions of global doom have been heard throughout history and have a bad habit of not coming true.

A balanced point of view also means something else. There are many groups and individuals who want to wipe out all types of pollution but in ways that promise to harm their fellow humans. They often call for stringent measures that are economically impossible for many families, cities, and businesses to follow and that threaten to cost thousands, perhaps millions, of workers their jobs. A balanced point of view calls for you to support methods that will preserve the waters and keep them clean, but will do so without making life intolerable for countless people. Such measures can be—and are being—found. Like your balanced point of view, they, too, provide a balance—this one between the rights and needs of nature and our own rights and needs.

What to Do with What You Learn

While it's necessary to expand your knowledge in every way possible, it's just as necessary not to keep what you learn to yourself. You should pass it on to others. The more people you can interest in water pollution, the greater the chances will be that another someone will join in efforts to alleviate or end the problem.

You can start with everyone at home—your parents, brothers and sisters, visiting relatives, and friends. See what you can do to get a discussion started at the dinner table one night. Or right after there has been a television documentary or news items on some new water problem.

Next, there are your friends outside your home. At school, why not get some of them together and present a classroom program on the subject? Or why not present it at a school assembly or a church or club meeting? Do everything you can to make it interesting with stories, photographs, charts, drawings, and, if possible, VCR recordings of scenes shot with a camcorder.

And you can go a step further. Ask local adult organizations—say, the Rotary or Kiwanis Club—if they would like to have their memberships see the program. They'll probably be interested because it promises to be something different from the programs and talks they usually feature.

If you do present your program on a number of occasions, be sure to clip and save the latest newspaper and magazine articles on water pollution. They'll help you keep your program material up-to-date.

How About the Written Word?

Are you interested in writing? Are you perhaps thinking that you'd like to go into journalism one day? If so, get to work and write an article—or a series of articles—for your school newspaper. Or your hometown or neighborhood newspaper. Don't be afraid of approaching the local paper. You'll very likely find that the editor is interested and impressed, especially if your article is about a local water problem, something that will have particular meaning for the readers. But be sure that the material is logically presented and as well and as clearly written as you can make it.

Take Political Action

While we're on the subject of writing, you should—now and certainly later as an adult—pick up your pen or get to your computer when you learn that Congress, your state legislature, or your local government is planning to enact a water measure. Let your representatives know what you think of the measure—whether you're for or against it, and *why*—and urge them to vote accordingly.

When you reach voting age—and for all the years that follow—study your local, state, and national representatives so that you can cast a wise ballot. Learn what their attitudes are toward all environmental matters. Do they seem to care about clean water or do they just give it lip service? Do they support proposed measures that are for or against cleansing or conserving the waters? Or do they do nothing at all? Vote for those whom you come to trust and whose views match yours.

Be sure to urge your Congressional representatives to support the country's participation in international programs seeking to reduce or end all types of pollution. Local programs help small areas. State and national programs help larger and larger areas. International programs help the world.

Watch Your Behavior

Once you become an advocate for clean water, you'll have to be very careful of your own behavior. You'll not be able to let yourself do anything that runs contrary to your views; otherwise, your friends are going to brand you a hypocrite. And so, when you go with a group to the beach or hold a picnic alongside a river or a lake, make sure that you don't leave the place littered with rubbish that can make its way into the water. You'll be the one who has to take the lead in finding a litter bin or packing the stuff to take home for disposal.

And you'll have to do more. The following rules should never be far from mind:

When you're out in a boat and have a soft drink, don't toss the can overboard—and, under no circumstances, ever toss one of those six-pack rings into the water. Remember, they're killers.

If you change the oil in your own car, don't let the used oil flow away into a drain or a gutter, there to find its way into your town's water system. Pour it into a container and take it to a disposal or recycling facility. Your city government office or local garbage collection agency can tell you where the facility is located. If your town has a pickup system for recycling, you can simply leave the container out at your front curb on collection day.

The same holds true for old paint. Don't dump it in a gutter. Take care of it through recycling.

In fact, don't toss anything in a gutter, not even if it's the smallest thing you can think of. A gum wrapper tossed away may seem like nothing, but it becomes something—and something very big—when it is joined by millions of others. If any of your friends doubt this, just remind them of the 1.3 million cigarette butts that were collected during the 1995 beach cleanup by the Center for Marine Conservation. They were all small and dropped one at a time.

Conserve water, even in times when your area is not being visited by a drought. Don't let the kitchen faucet or the garden hose run for long minutes just because you're too lazy to turn it off. Don't use a ton of water in the shower just because it makes you feel good. Remember, water is a precious resource that is being used by more and more people every year as the world's population increases. It should be treated as the precious thing it is.

An Ounce of Prevention

Much attention today is being given to the waters that are already polluted. Billions of dollars are being spent to return them to good health. These efforts deserve your wholehearted support. But there is something of equal importance that you should do—give your attention to waters that are still clean.

If you work to protect them from becoming polluted, you'll achieve two results. First, you'll keep pollution from spreading and, second, you'll save the waters from becoming poisoned and costing a truckload of money to nurse back to health. You'll be making a very old and wise saying come true: *An ounce of prevention is worth a pound of cure.*

But just what can you do to safeguard a healthy body of water? Many things. For example:

Suppose that you vacation at a favorite lake or seaside where there is a group of volunteers who work to keep its beaches and water clean by picking up trash and asking visitors always to place their rubbish in litter bins or carry it away. Take some time off from having fun and lend them a hand.

Or suppose there is a stretch of sea near you whose coral formations are being threatened by refuse or disturbed by intrusive sports activities (such as powerboating). And suppose there is a group working to protect the coral and its sea life by urging the state to set it aside as a sanctuary against further harm. Again, lend them a hand.

One of the best services you can perform is to join the thousands of volunteers who participate in the annual cleanup by the Center for Marine Conservation. Watch your local newspaper for an announcement of when the next cleanup is scheduled. If you wish to contact the Center, its address is 1725 DeSales N.W., Suite 500, Washington, D.C. 20036. The telephone number is (202) 429-5609. The FAX number is (202) 872-0619.

You may be very enthusiastic at this moment about curbing water pollution. But, since we all know that many interests come and go, make an effort to keep your enthusiasm high as the years pass. It's important that you do so because, even though you have the power as a young person to help change things, you will have far more power once you reach adulthood. You may then have a job in private industry or hold a public position that will enable you to urge or perhaps formulate wise water measures in your city or state, or even at the national level. Or you may be a member or the leader of an organization or club that can influence the public's attitude toward wise water use. There are untold ways in which you might become a figure able to make a significant contribution to the cleansing of the world's waters.

And so never forget that fighting water pollution—or any environmental danger—is a lifelong job. The best to you in carrying it out.

BIBLIOGRAPHY

Books

Asimov, Isaac and Pohl, Frederik. *Our Angry Earth*. New York: Tom Doherty Associates, 1991.

Aylesworth, Thomas G. *This Vital Air, This Vital Water: Man's Environmental Crisis* (revised edition). Chicago: Rand McNally, 1973.

Bast, Joseph L.; Hill, Peter J.; and Rue, Richard C. *Eco-Sanity: A Common-Sense Guide to Environmentalism*. Lanham, Maryland: Madison Books, 1994.

Batten, Louis J. *Weather in Your Life*. New York: W. H. Freeman, 1983.

Brown, Lester R., Editor. *State of the World 1990: A Worldwatch Institute Report on Progress Toward a Sustainable Society*. New York: W. W. Norton, 1990.

—— *State of the World 1993: A Worldwatch Institute Report on Progress Toward a Sustainable Society*. New York: W. W. Norton, 1993.

———— *State of the World 1995: A Worldwatch Institute Report on Progress Toward a Sustainable Society*. New York: W. W. Norton, 1995.

———— *State of the World 1996: A Worldwatch Institute Report on Progress Toward a Sustainable Society*. New York: W. W. Norton, 1996.

Clark, Robert B. *Marine Pollution* (2nd revised edition). New York: Oxford University Press, 1989.

Colborn, Theo; Dumanoski, Dianne; and Myers, John Peterson. *Our Stolen Future*. New York: Dutton, 1996.

Dolan, Edward F. *Drought: The Past, Present, and Future Enemy*. New York: Franklin Watts, 1990.

———— *The American Wilderness and Its Future: Conservation Versus Use*. New York: Franklin Watts, 1992.

———— with Scariano, Margaret M. *Nuclear Waste: The 10,000-Year Challenge*. New York: Franklin Watts, 1990.

Dorland's Illustrated Medical Dictionary (23rd edition). Philadelphia: W. B. Saunders, 1953.

Earle, Sylvia A. *Sea Change: A Message of the Oceans*. New York: G. P. Putnam's Sons, 1995.

Gorman, Martha. *Environmental Hazards: Marine Pollution*. Santa Barbara, California: ABC-CLIO, 1993.

Miller, E. Willard and Miller, Ruby. *Water Quality and Availability*. Santa Barbara, California: ABC-CLIO, 1992.

Moorcraft, Colin. *Must the Seas Die?* Boston: Gambit, 1973.

Myers, Norman. *The GAIA Atlas of Future Worlds: Challenge and Opportunity in an Age of Change*. New York: Anchor Books, Doubleday, 1990.

Naar, Jon. *Design for a Livable Planet: How You Can Help Clean Up the Environment*. New York: Harper & Row, 1990.

Postel, Sandra. *Last Oasis: Facing Water Scarcity*. New York: W. W. Norton, 1992.

Robinson, Marilynne. *Mother Country*. New York: Farrar, Straus & Giroux, 1989.

Periodicals

Adler, Jerry. "Troubled Waters," *Newsweek*, April 16, 1990.

Chafee, John. "Preparing for the Next Century," *EPA Journal*, April 1, 1995.

Faeth, Paul. "Building the Case for Sustainable Agriculture," *Environment*, January 1, 1994.

Griffin, Joel. "Water Management Is Vital," *Asian Business Review*, August 1, 1995.

Hair, Jay. "NWF Acts to Save Clean Water Act from Assault by Congress," *International Wildlife*, July 1, 1995.

Kerry, John F. Senator. "Omnibus Budget Reconciliation Act —Conference Report," *Congressional Record*, October 17, 1990.

"Laws and the Environment," *Earth Explorer*, February 1, 1995.

Mohammadioun, Mina and Coronado, Julia Lynn. "Pollution Prevention: A Paradigm Shift in Environmental Management," *Texas Business Review*, June 1, 1995.

Northoff, Erwin. "The Suffocating Black Sea," *World Press Review*, August, 1995.

Pittendreigh, Jr., W. "Bridging the Clean Water Gap," *Environmental Action*, April 1, 1994.

Postel, Sandra. "Earth's Rivers Are Running Dry," *USA Today Magazine*, November 1, 1995.

"Surface-Water Pollution," *Earth Explorer*, February 1, 1995.

Toufexis, Anatasia. "The Dirty Seas," *Time*, August 1, 1988.

Tufts, Craig. "What Can You Do For Clean Water?" *National Wildlife*, October 1, 1995.

Wirtz, Ronald. "Federal and State Government Assistance Programs," *Business Journal Serving Greater Milwaukee*," July 29, 1995.

Newspapers and Newspaper Services

Barnum, Alex. "Fishing With Cyanide Destroys Reefs," *San Francisco Chronicle*, October 28, 1995.

Diamond, Randy. "Tourists Avoiding Jersey Like the Plague," *San Francisco Examiner*, August 14, 1988.

Drozdiak, William. "Onetime 'Sewer of Europe,' the Rhine Is Reborn." *San Francisco Chronicle* (from *Washington Post*), April 1, 1996.

Fitzgerald, Randy. "The Case of the Poisoned Wildlife Refuge," *Reader's Digest*, October, 1987.

Kanamine, Linda. "Under-treated Water Flows to 50 Million," *USA Today*, July 28, 1994.

Kass, John. "Florida's Great Everglades Is Dying a Little Each Year," *San Francisco Examiner* (from *Chicago Tribune*), October 21, 1990.

Martin, Glen. "Troubled Waters," *San Francisco Chronicle*, March 26, 1995.

Miller, Ken. "Rolex, Sports Car Among Tons of Trash Scooped from Beaches," Gannett News Service, June 21, 1995.

Mitchell, Alison. "Clinton Signs a Bill on Water Contaminants," *New York Times*, August 7, 1996.

Murphy, Kim. "7 Years Later, Work to Clean Up Exxon Spill Goes On," *San Francisco Chronicle* (from *Los Angeles Times*), June 28, 1996.

Nusser, Nancy. "As Water Crisis Worsens, Mexico City Becomes a Sinkhole," *San Francisco Chronicle* (from Cox News Service), January 27, 1996.

Perlman, David. "Heavy Lead Pollution Found in Sea Otters," *San Francisco Chronicle*, October 11, 1990.

Petit, Charles. "Just Add Water," *San Francsico Chronicle*, November 26, 1995.

"17,365 Waterways Polluted, EPA Says," *San Francisco Chronicle*, June 14, 1989.

Shabecoff, Philip. "An Emergence of Political Will on Acid Rain," *New York Times*, February 19, 1989.

Stammer, Larry B. "Offshore Oil Rigs Come Under Tougher Anti-Pollution Rules," *Los Angeles Times*, August 25, 1992.

Taylor, Humphrey. "Children Deeply Concerned about Environmental Problems," Gannett News Service, April 3, 1994.

Tyson, Rae. "Cleaner Waterways Just a Drop in the Bucket—Despite Success Stories, Problems Still Run Deep," *USA Today*, May 31, 1994.

Yearwood, Pauline. "Let All Be Fed—But How?" *Greater Phoenix Jewish News*, April 21, 1995.

Special Publications

Compilation of Selected Water Resources and Environmental Laws (Prepared for the Committee on Public Works and Transportation, U.S. House of Representatives). Washington, D.C.: U.S. Government Printing Office, 1993.

Creating a Government That Works Better and Costs Less. Washington, D.C.: U.S. Environmental Protection Agency, 1993.

Current Industrial Reports: Pollution Abatement Costs and Expenditures. Washington, D.C.: U.S. Department of Commerce, 1993.

Guide to Federal Water Quality Programs and Information. Washington, D.C.: U.S. Environmental Protection Agency, 1993.

The National Parks Index, 1989. Washington, D.C.: U.S. Department of the Interior, 1989.

National Water Summary, 1990–91: Hydrologic Events and Stream Water Quality. Washington, D.C.: U.S. Geological Survey, 1993.

Oil Pollution Act of 1990. Washington, D.C.: U.S. Government Printing Office, undated.

Television and Radio Transcripts

"Proposed Overhaul of the 1972 Clean Water Act." WNET, New York: McNeil/Lehrer Newshour, May 11, 1995.

"Rio Grande and Its Dependents in Trouble," Weekend Edition, National Public Radio, November 6, 1993.

General References

The American Almanac 1994–1995: Statistical Abstract of the United States (114th edition). Austin, Texas: Reference Press, 1994.

Barnes & Noble New American Encyclopedia. Volumes 2, 5, 14, 15, 20. Grolier Incorporated, 1991.

Information Please Almanac, 1995 (4th edition). New York: Houghton Mifflin, 1995

INDEX

L

SMYTHE GAMBRELL LIBRARY
WESTMINSTER SCHOOLS
1424 WEST PACES FERRY RD NW
ATLANTA GEORGIA 30327